WHAT IS POLITICAL PHILOSOPHY?

What Is Political Philosophy?

CHARLES LARMORE

PRINCETON UNIVERSITY PRESS

PRINCETON & OXFORD

Published by Princeton University Press
41 William Street, Princeton, New Jersey 08540
6 Oxford Street, Woodstock, Oxfordshire OX20 1TR

press.princeton.edu

Library of Congress Cataloging-in-Publication Data
Names: Larmore, Charles, 1950– author.
Title: What is political philosophy? / Charles Larmore.
Description: Princeton, New Jersey: Princeton University Press, 2020. |
Includes bibliographical references and index.
Identifiers: LCCN 2019041504 (print) | LCCN 2019041505 (ebook) |
ISBN 9780691179148 (hardback) | ISBN 9780691200873 (ebook)
Subjects: LCSH: Political science—Philosophy. | Political ethics. |
Legitimacy of governments.
Classification: LCC JA79 .L38 2020 (print) | LCC JA79 (ebook) | DDC
320.01—dc23
LC record available at https://lccn.loc.gov/2019041504
LC ebook record available at https://lccn.loc.gov/2019041505
British Library Cataloging-in-Publication Data is available

Editorial: Rob Tempio and Matt Rohal
Production Editorial: Natalie Baan
Jacket Design: Chris Ferrante
Production: Danielle Amatucci
Publicity: Katie Lewis, Amy Stewart, and Alyssa Sanford
Copyeditor: Hank Southgate

This book has been composed in Arno

Printed on acid-free paper. ∞

Printed in the United States of America

10 9 8 7 6 5 4 3 2 1

CONTENTS

v

ACKNOWLEDGMENTS

I AM VERY grateful to the following people who have discussed with me the material in this volume and commented on various parts of the manuscript: Derek Bowman, Eva Buddeberg, G. A. Cohen, David Estlund, Rainer Forst, Wilfried Hinsch, Daniel Layman, Matt Sleat, Kevin Vallier, and Michael Williams. I am particularly indebted to Jerry Cohen, who, shortly before his tragic death, gave me an extensive set of valuable comments on a version of chapter 1 (and not just on the part devoted to his own work). I also want to thank Rob Tempio, my editor at Princeton University Press, for his encouragement and advice, as well as two anonymous referees for their helpful criticisms and suggestions. I thank as well Hank Southgate for his expert copyediting.

Earlier versions of the three chapters of this book have appeared elsewhere, but they have been significantly revised and much expanded. I would like to thank the publishers of the original publications for their kind permission to reuse them here.

Chapter 1, "The Relation between Political and Moral Philosophy," was originally published under the title "What Is Political Philosophy?," *Journal of Moral Philosophy* 10, no. 3 (2012): 276–306. Reprinted by permission of Koninklijke Brill NV.

Chapter 2, "The Truth in Political Realism," was originally published in *Politics Recovered: Essays on Realist Political Theory*, ed. Matt Sleat (New York: Columbia University Press, 2018), 27–48. Reprinted by permission of Columbia University Press. Chapter 3, "Political Liberalism and Legitimacy," was originally published under the title "Political Liberalism: Its Motivations and Goals," in *Oxford Studies in Political Philosophy* 1 (Oxford: Oxford University Press, 2015): 63–88. Reprinted by permission of Oxford University Press.

WHAT IS POLITICAL PHILOSOPHY?

Introduction

PHILOSOPHY TENDS NATURALLY to turn its attention to the nature of philosophy itself. This has been evident ever since Plato, who believed he had to understand how Socrates's way of addressing the key questions of life differed from that of the Sophists if he was to work out his own conceptions of knowledge, virtue, and happiness. The self-reflexivity of philosophy does not stem from a search for certainty. The idea has not been, at least at bottom, that in reflecting on the capacities of mind and guiding interests these questions call upon we will be able to devise appropriate methods for answering them once and for all. That may have been Descartes's hope. But it is surely an illusion. The motivation lies instead in a desire essential to the very enterprise of philosophy.

As both Plato and Aristotle remarked, philosophy begins in wonder. Its starting point is not this or that particular problem that interrupts our everyday routine, but rather the feeling that a whole dimension of our dealings with things, if not indeed the world itself, has ceased to make sense as it once seemed to do. To think philosophically has therefore always meant to stand back from ordinary concerns and seek the larger picture. Its ultimate aim is to arrive at a broad understanding of how everything fits together in one way or another. One need not suppose that everything does so without tensions, conflicts, or even discontinuities. Reality may not be all of a piece. But this idea of an encompassing whole does have to include an idea of itself. That means, it has to include an account of the proper way to go about figuring out how the different parts of our experience interrelate. Philosophy aims to bring hidden presuppositions into view, to achieve a fully perspicuous grasp of all that is involved in our thinking about the world and our place in it, not least when we are engaged in precisely this radical kind of reflection. Even if one concludes, as Nietzsche did, that creativity depends on a certain amount of blindness or forgetting, this fact itself will form part of such a comprehensive vision.

Other disciplines of thought, such as the various sciences, are defined by their particular domain of inquiry. They are generally content as well to operate within a framework of settled assumptions and results, except at those rare times when, turning "philosophical," they feel the need to re-examine basic elements of what has hitherto been taken for granted. Of course, philosophy, too, often focuses on specific subjects: there is the philosophy of art, the philosophical study of conditionals or punishment. Yet a sense of an encompassing whole remains on the horizon. It is at work in the common recognition that different philosophical problems invariably interconnect and that the way one approaches a given topic is therefore philosophically as important as the conclusions one happens to draw. In its aspiration to an understanding of the whole of reality, philosophy is alone. Physics, for instance, makes no such pretension. It is physicalism that claims we must look to physics for this sort of understanding, and physicalism is a philosophical doctrine. Because then philosophy seeks in the end to grasp how everything fits together, it is naturally led, whether its object happens to be some particular topic or reality as a whole, to reflect on how it must itself proceed if it is to accomplish its task. Its primary concern lies accordingly with the core concepts and principles that should shape our thinking about whatever domain it is considering. This ambition is a constant even though philosophy takes, to be sure, different historical forms, depending on the reigning beliefs about the world and ourselves.

The present book is a book in political philosophy. But for the reasons I have mentioned, it is also a book about political philosophy. In fact, reflection about the nature of political philosophy—about what are the central problems it must grapple with and the core concepts it must explore—occupies a large part of the book. Only in the third and final chapter do I turn in any sustained way to first-order questions. There I lay out a conception, a fundamentally liberal conception, of the basic shape political society should take today. Only then do I begin, as it were, to practice what I preach.

I have devoted so much attention to the nature of political philosophy because I believe that, properly understood, it differs from moral philosophy far more deeply than is generally supposed. As a rule, political philosophy is seen, if only implicitly, as part of the broader discipline of moral philosophy. The right and the good, both in themselves and in their various ramifications, form the subject of moral philosophy. Political philosophy, as usually practiced, sets about its work within this framework. It bases itself on those principles of morality it regards as governing, not our individual relationships to others, but instead the functioning of society as a whole in order then to determine, in the light of social realities, the sorts of institutions in which they would be best embodied. In essence, political philosophy has therefore proceeded by applying what it takes to be moral truths about the makeup of the good society to the exigencies of the real world. A contemporary example is the way that, ever since the publication of John Rawls's *A Theory of Justice* (1971), political philosophy in the Anglo-American world has come to seem devoted primarily to developing one conception of social justice after another.

In recent years, others too have complained about this habit of conceiving of political philosophy as applied moral philosophy. I discuss their views in the course of the first two chapters. Here I want to outline my own basis for rejecting that conception, a basis that is importantly different from theirs.

Pervasive conflict about what should count as the terms of social cooperation and thus the need for authoritative, enforceable rules constitute the elementary facts of political life. Yet among the most enduring and polarizing sources of social discord is disagreement about the nature of the right and the good, about more specific moral questions, and in particular about the features of the good or just society. One of the roles of a conception of justice is to show how to adjudicate conflicts among the members of society, yet the nature of justice is itself an abiding object of controversy. Disagreements of this sort, moreover, often consist in more than people merely holding different views. They can result when reasonable people— that is, people reasoning in good faith and to the best of their abilities—reflect about what it is to live well. It is a common experience, at least in those parts of the world in which people enjoy freedom of thought and expression, that reasoning about ethical matters, once it goes beyond platitudes and seeks some precision, is as likely to drive us apart as to bring us together. Sometimes these conflicts are between individuals (we can even turn out to be at odds with ourselves). But sometimes they arise between groups following different moral or religious traditions, and though these traditions generally have their own internal controversies, such conflicts in the absence of laws to handle them can render social cooperation difficult or even impossible.

This, then, is why political philosophy is not properly a province of moral philosophy. If its fundamental task is to determine the kind of political order that can justifiably impose authoritative rules for handling the major conflicts in society, then it must reckon with the fact that such conflicts include precisely those arising from reasonable disagreement about the elements of morality itself. It follows, as I explain in this book, that legitimacy, not distributive justice as typically supposed today, ought to be the primary object of political philosophy. For legitimacy has to do with the conditions under which enforceable rules may be justifiably imposed on the members of a society. Only if a system of political rule is more or less legitimate should it make sense to ask what principles of justice it ought to establish. Though others as well have rejected the idea of political philosophy as applied moral philosophy, they have not relied on the sort of argument just summarized or given it the prominence it deserves.

The phenomenon of reasonable disagreement is a constant theme in this book. The idea can seem paradoxical, and not only because the philosophical tradition has so frequently assumed that reason, if exercised well, leads inevitably to convergence of opinion. It can also seem that reasonable people, if they discover that other people, whom they consider equally reasonable, disagree with them about some issue, would backtrack and cease to hold their belief, so that reasonable disagreement would vanish. That this is not so is one of the things I show in the detailed analysis of the phenomenon given in chapter 3. Disagreement can persist among reasonable people because being reasonable is a matter of how we go on from our respective starting points, which may be very different.

Before the modern era, reasonable disagreement about moral questions was rarely acknowledged as something to be expected. Disagreement itself was, of course, all too familiar. But the general presumption was that it came about through faulty inference or inadequate evidence on the part of some or all of those involved. As I indicated, the dominant idea was that the exercise of reason leads, here as elsewhere, ultimately to unanimity. Not even the various forms of ancient skepticism posed a real challenge to this view. For they generally supposed that reason is at one in determining what is dubitable (and so warranting suspension of judgment) or what is merely probable (and so warranting tentative endorsement). There was, moreover, in societies under the sway of religious orthodoxies a limited experience of feeling free in discussion or even in one's own reflection to follow an ethical line of thought wherever it might lead, including into conflict with accepted opinion. Tradition and oppression kept the phenomenon submerged.

Things began to change in early modern times. The Renaissance brought the rediscovery of the unsuspected diversity of Greek and Roman thought. (Dante could so confidently call Aristotle "il maestro di color che sanno" because he was like all his contemporaries largely ignorant of the range of ancient philosophy.[1]) Later with the Reformation came the exalting of individual conscience and, as a result, the fragmentation of religious unity. As the ability of the Church to impose discipline began to wane and people felt more and more able to reason for themselves about what a Christian life requires, they also

---

1. Dante, *Inferno*, IV.131 ("the master of those who know").

grew to realize that others are apt to arrive at convictions opposed to their own. Innovative thinkers such as Montaigne and Hobbes, neither of them religiously inclined themselves, saw the phenomenon more broadly. They pointed out how easily reasoning about the right and the good in general can lead to disagreement not only with others but even with oneself, "reasons having," as Montaigne observed, "hardly any other foundation than experience, and the diversity of human events presenting us with innumerable examples of every possible import [*à toute sorte de formes*]."[2] Their generalization anticipated later developments. For as ethical thinking in much of society has gradually abandoned the framework of religious belief, the extent to which moral questions can be expected to provoke reasonable disagreement has become ever more far-reaching.

Though this expectation is a pervasive feature of our culture, its significance for the self-understanding of political philosophy has not, I have suggested, been rightly appreciated. For it ought to be seen as signaling that political philosophy should enjoy a far greater autonomy from moral philosophy than it has usually been given. Disagreement about moral questions is a principal source of social conflict and indeed one that can tear societies apart. This is immediately evident from the religious wars that devastated Europe in the sixteenth and seventeenth centuries, wars fueled by opposing conceptions of what it is to live a Christian life.[3] But examples also abound in later times. The nineteenth-century social revolutions in France

2. Michel de Montaigne, *Les Essais*, ed. M. Villey (Paris: PUF, 1999), II.17 ("De la présomption"), 655.

3. It is generally believed that at least five million people (20 percent of the population) died as a result of the Thirty Years' War (1618–48) in the German Empire alone. See Peter H. Wilson, *The Thirty Years War* (Cambridge, MA: Harvard University Press, 2009), 787.

(1830, 1848, 1871) and elsewhere were fueled by conflicting ideas about property rights and about the meaning and relative importance of freedom and equality. And today, clashing views about what it is for a nation to maintain a sense of its own identity, about whether its chief concern should be to protect itself from foreign influences that undermine its accustomed way of life or instead to change inherited traditions as it engages with other nations in relations of mutual benefit, are putting the Western democracies under terrible strain.

Precisely because controversies of this sort involve positions that appear reasonable to their adherents, the social conflicts they generate cannot be adjudicated simply by appealing to supposed truths of morality. Each side is already doing just that. Instead, an answer has to be devised to an essentially political question that forms no part of moral philosophy. It is this: Given disagreement about the morally appropriate response to some social problem demanding an *authoritative* solution, that is, a solution that will receive widespread acceptance, under what conditions may *enforceable* rules to handle the problem be *legitimately* imposed on the members of a society? It can turn out that the rules imposed are those favored by one of the contending positions. Yet this does not mean that the moral views it embodies have been "applied" to the case at hand. The rules are authoritative, not because they are widely believed to be morally valid, but because they have been instituted by a political system that is widely held to be (more or less) legitimate. Political, as opposed to moral, questions are questions having to do with power and its legitimate exercise.

Now although the phenomenon of reasonable disagreement has not shaped as it should the self-understanding of political philosophy in general, it has in fact played a significant role in the formation of modern liberalism. One need only think of the prominent place that ideas of toleration have always occupied in liberal thought. These ideas emerged in early modern times as the realization took hold that people thinking sincerely and carefully about matters of faith but also more generally about the makeup of the human good are prone to disagree, often in virtue of differing about what it is in such cases to reason well. Taming the passions and settling conflicts among discordant interests had long been seen as the key problems political rule must solve if it is to secure the conditions of social cooperation. It had also been believed that this is possible only if the members of society by and large share a common conception of the ultimate ends of life. Yet now there had emerged a more profound problem, which called into question not only the latter belief but the very basis of political rule. If there is disagreement among reasonable people about religious and ethical matters and about their implications for the organization of society, it seemed unclear what system of rule a political regime can justifiably exercise over them, a justification having to be offered if it is to claim to be legitimate.

Such is the problem that stands at the origin of the liberal tradition. Though the term "liberalism" appeared only at the beginning of the nineteenth century, the roots of this tradition reach several centuries further back. Indeed, I should note incidentally that in this book I use the term, not in the partisan sense it often assumes in contemporary politics, but rather to designate a broader political orientation that gives primacy to individual freedom and equality. Thus, among the sources of the liberal tradition in this sense were early modern conceptions of religious toleration, and they often involved, as in the writings of thinkers such as Bodin, Hobbes, Spinoza, and Bayle, the effort to look beyond deep religious and ethical disagreements and find in more abstract concerns such as self-interest, a regard for the favorable opinion of others, or a basic sense of what is right and fair the source of political principles by which people can, despite such differences, live and work together to their mutual advantage. Certainly, the most influential of these early figures was Locke. But liberal thought did not culminate with him. The project of working out a common basis of political association amid reasonable disagreement about the human good went on to take new forms in subsequent centuries.

Along with Kant and Mill, the two preeminent figures in later times, Locke shares nonetheless two distinctive assumptions, which typify what in this book I call "classical liberalism." Not only did they regard reasonable disagreement about the good as the cardinal problem facing the possibility of legitimate rule, but they also sought a solution to this problem in different versions of what is effectively an ethics of individualism. By that I mean an ethics that gives paramount value to thinking for oneself and to working out on one's own how one will live. Their common thought was that since any substantial conception of the good, any particular religion or cultural tradition, is thus valuable only if it was or would be chosen from a standpoint of open-minded and critical reflection, political legitimacy should no longer be based, as in the past, on inevitably controversial conceptions of this sort. Political rule should instead be justified by appeal to this individualist ethic itself, to—as Locke, Kant, and Mill would have said respectively— the fallibilist, autonomous, or experimental attitude toward life that ought to form people's deepest self-understanding. For it will move people to endorse principles of political life that, without relying on specific conceptions of the human good, endow them with the freedoms, powers, and protections necessary to exercise this individualist approach to life. Whence such principles as liberty of conscience, freedom of association, equality of opportunity, political equality, and even the right to a social minimum that have become characteristic of liberal thought. Much of the subsequent liberal tradition has proceeded along these lines.

However, this individualist ethic in its various forms has itself turned out to be an object of reasonable disagreement. Ever since the Romantic era's rehabilitation of the importance of tradition and belonging, the idea that we should always maintain a distanced, questioning stance toward inherited ways of life has come to seem to many, and not without reason, to be too one-sided a demand. Not all our commitments can be elective, since our choices depend ultimately on a sense of what is good and right that is taken for granted. Critical reflection is in reality but one value among many, and giving it supreme authority can blind us to the role of shared customs, ties of language and place, and religious faith in shaping the very understanding of good and ill through which we make the choices we do. This is the core of the frequent complaint of the last two centuries that liberalism's individualist ethic dissolves social bonds and impoverishes our moral thinking. Such an ethic is not itself a substantial conception of the human good, but instead an attitude purporting to govern the acceptance of any such conception. Yet it is no less apt to prove a subject of dispute and conflict among people reasoning in good faith and to the best of their abilities about what it is to live well.

In response to this situation, liberal thought has gone in two separate directions. One current has continued to rely on some version of an individualist view of life. Seeking now more explicitly than before to ground basic liberal principles on a comprehensive, if also controversial, idea of human flourishing, this form of liberalism has thus become what its defenders themselves often call a "perfectionist" doctrine. An opposing current, commonly called "political liberalism"—it is the approach I myself favor—takes more seriously the persistence of reasonable disagreement about individualist values. It seeks a basis of political association that is independent of them as well as of religious beliefs and ethical ideals. It does so because it believes that the guiding conviction of liberal thinking really lies at a deeper level. This conviction has to do, in my view, not so much with the way we should live our own lives, as with how we should treat others. It turns upon a particular idea of respect for persons, having to do with the use or threat of force. The conception of political legitimacy it serves to justify will be formulated as follows. The fundamental principles of political society ought, precisely because they are coercive in nature, also to be such that those subject to them should be able to see from their perspective reason to endorse them, assuming a commitment—which some may in fact not have—to basing political association on principles that can meet with the reasonable agreement of all citizens.

Since I discuss this idea of respect at length in chapter 3, I will not go further into it now except to note one obvious point. The idea is clearly moral in character. Thus, the liberal conception of legitimacy it defines rests on moral grounds. This fact may appear to belie my rejection of the view of political philosophy as applied moral philosophy. Yet as I explain in the first two chapters, every conception of political legitimacy has to have some moral foundation, since it aims to identify the conditions under which a system of political rule may justifiably wield power over those it governs. The question is whether this moral foundation consists in a broad religious or ethical vision of the human good and the just society or whether instead it focuses strictly on the problem of justifying the exercise of coercive power. For this is an essentially political problem. It has no place in moral philosophy, which is concerned with the nature of the good and the right, with our means of grasping and acting on them, but not with the social conflicts that arise when reasonable people disagree about such matters. A political philosophy that regards the solution of this problem as the basis of the rest it proposes is not therefore in any meaningful sense "applied moral philosophy." Liberalism, particularly when it takes the form of "political liberalism," proceeds in just that way and precisely because it recognizes how socially divisive, in the absence of state authority, following one's moral convictions can prove.

It is true, as these remarks suggest, that liberal thinkers have always been eager to find fundamental political principles on which people can agree. But nothing could be more wrong than to suppose that the liberal vision of society is one essentially of moral consensus.[4] That would be to miss the problem to which consensus is the intended solution as well as to misunderstand the nature of the consensus in question. Liberals have looked for bases of agreement precisely because they have been so keenly aware of the persistent disagreements about religious and ethical questions that make for extensive and sometimes destructive social conflict. The basic principles on which liberalism seeks agreement are not, moreover, principles people are presumed to share already, but rather principles it holds that there is reason for them to accept. Classical liberals knew

---

4. The misconception is all too frequent. See, for instance, Raymond Geuss in "Liberalism and Its Discontents," *Political Theory* 30, no. 3 (June 2002): 326: "One sometimes hears the claim that liberalism differs from other political philosophies through its recognition of the plurality of potentially valuable modes of life. This is a highly misleading assertion…. The multiple forms of life that liberalism recognizes are always assumed to be embedded in an overriding consensus that has a latent moral significance."

full well that many members of society were not antecedently disposed to endorse an individualist view of life. The same goes for the principle of respect for persons, as will become apparent when I present my version of political liberalism later in this book. No doubt, liberal thinkers have often been too sanguine about the extent to which people who do not yet accept the basis of a liberal political order could come to be able to see, from their perspective, reason to adopt it. This was clearly the case with the representatives of classical liberalism. I, by contrast, acknowledge the point at length in chapters 2 and 3 of this book. Every conception of political legitimacy, however inclusive it may seek to be, also excludes by virtue of resting on moral and factual beliefs that some people from their point of view are bound to see reason to reject.

Reasonable disagreement about the good and the right, in all its depth and breadth, has therefore always stood at the center of liberalism's attention. I could not agree more with Edmund Fawcett, who recounts the history of the liberal tradition as the development of four cardinal ideas—"acknowledgement of inescapable material and ethical conflict within society, distrust of power, faith in human progress, and respect for people whatever they think and whoever they are"—though I am increasingly skeptical about the validity of the third.[5] At the same time, I would caution against supposing that liberalism has an essence in any substantial sense. Like all intellectual traditions, it has developed and undergone profound changes over time. One such change that I have not touched on is liberalism's only gradual acceptance of democracy. Another change that I have

---

5. Edmund Fawcett, *Liberalism: The Life of an Idea* (Princeton, NJ: Princeton University Press, 2014), xix. Some of my reasons for skepticism about human progress can be found at the end of chapter 3.

mentioned lies in the critique of classical liberalism at the hands of political liberalism.

However, the tendency to reasonable disagreement about ethical questions has not, I have already observed, been integrated into the self-understanding of political philosophy itself. All too often, political philosophy has taken its point of departure to be the moral principles that should determine the workings of society as a whole. One example is the reliance of classical liberalism upon an individualist view of life. Another is the extent to which political philosophy in our day threatens to become synonymous with the theory of social justice. What this ethics-centered approach has missed is the fact that the social conflicts that political philosophy must explore the ways of solving can stem in great part from moral disputes about how society should be best organized, disputes in which each side can from its point of view claim to have good reasons for its position. To an important extent, moral views are not so much the solution as the problem. This means that the fundamental political question, as well as the fundamental question for political philosophy, has to be the conditions under which authoritative, enforceable rules for handling such conflicts can justifiably be instituted. Legitimacy should be political philosophy's primary concern, justice figuring only derivatively.

It may seem that I am in effect presenting liberalism, particularly in the more careful form of political liberalism, as the only political conception compatible with the real nature of political philosophy. This is not so. True, a distinctive feature of liberal thought has been its concern with how widespread reasonable disagreement can be about various aspects of the human good. But its defining principles constitute a response to this problem, a response that is itself moral in character. It affirms in effect the value of people exercising their reason by their own best lights (individualist or not) even at the price of deep and widespread differences of opinion, since it holds that basic political principles ought to be such that citizens committed to mutual respect can, despite their disagreements, all see reason to endorse them. But different sorts of responses, drawing on different moral premises, are also possible. One might, for instance, conclude that if reasonable people differ so greatly about the nature of the right and the good, then this is a sign of man's fallen state and political rule should therefore be based, not on respect for individual reason, but instead on conformity to God's will. Liberal thought stands out from other traditions by its vivid sense of the fundamental political *problem* posed by reasonable disagreement about the good and the right. But the *solution* it proposes cannot claim to rise above all such disagreement.

If liberalism has seen more clearly than past conceptions the true task of political philosophy, that is because, as part of a reflective culture imbued with historical self-awareness, it has acquired a clearer view of the fundamental problems confronting political society. It has, as I explain in chapter 3, the character of a latecomer, having learned from the failings of earlier efforts to organize political life around some single core notion of a life lived well. However, its greater lucidity is not its justification. Its justification lies ultimately in the principle of respect for persons. And this principle, as I have just noted, is one that some people will see from their perspective reason to reject. Far from serving to legitimate a liberal political order, appreciation of the extent of reasonable disagreement entails recognizing that reasonable people can disagree about its legitimacy as well. As this book aims to show, there is indeed an intimate connection between the nature of political philosophy, properly understood, and the essential motivations of liberal thought.

Liberalism has played an important role in drawing attention to the way that moral convictions, however well thought out they may appear to their adherents, can easily diverge and lead to deep social conflict. Yet this tendency, though it shows why political and moral philosophy must be very different enterprises, extends more broadly than any particular conception of political society can fully accommodate.

If the final chapter of this book, whose theme is the nature of political philosophy, focuses on modern liberalism, it is in order to explain what is exactly the principle of political legitimacy it should be understood as propounding and why, even though some may see reason to reject it, it is the one that at least until now has best fit the modern world.

1

The Relation between Political
and Moral Philosophy

THE QUESTION IN the title of this book receives much less
attention than it deserves. Too often the domain of political
philosophy is defined by a series of classic texts (running from
Aristotle's *Politics*, through Hobbes's *Leviathan*, to Rawls's *A
Theory of Justice*) along with a conventional list of the topics to
be addressed—the acceptable limits of state action, the basis
of political obligation, the virtues of citizenship, and the nature
of social justice. Precisely this last topic, however, shows why
the question "What is political philosophy?" ought to have a
greater urgency. For justice is a topic that also belongs to moral
philosophy. How, therefore, are moral philosophy and political
philosophy to be distinguished? Both take as their subject the
principles by which we should live together in society. How
exactly do they differ? If justice—to invoke a traditional tag as
indisputable as it is uninformative—means giving everyone his
or her due (*suum cuique*), then what is it to fill in the import of
this phrase as a moral philosopher and to do so instead from
the standpoint of political philosophy?

18

These questions are not motivated by a general love of intellectual hygiene. I do not assume that the various areas of philosophy need always to be cleanly demarcated from one another in order to avoid contamination by alien concerns and influences. Rather, disciplines arise in response to problems, and the boundaries between them, when justified, reflect the extent to which they deal with different problems or handle what might seem to be similar problems from fundamentally different perspectives. Now political philosophy—to invoke what may also look like a vacuous definition—consists in systematic reflection about the nature and purposes of political life. The relation it has to moral philosophy depends therefore on how political philosophers, in tackling this subject, should position themselves with respect to the sphere of morality. There have been, broadly speaking, two competing conceptions.

1. Two Rival Conceptions

According to what has no doubt been the dominant view, political and moral philosophy do not differ essentially in their aims. Moral philosophy is supposedly the more general discipline, dealing as it does with the good and the right in all their manifold aspects. Political philosophy is held to form part of this larger enterprise, working out the class of moral principles that should govern, not our individual relationships to others, but rather the structure of society as a whole. One of its primary themes must therefore be social justice, and justice regarded as a moral ideal, conceived in abstraction from the realities of politics. Its aim is to specify the relations in which we ought ideally to stand to one another as members of society, possessed of the appropriate rights and responsibilities. Only once this basis is secured should political philosophy move on to take into account existing beliefs, motivations, and social conditions. The ideal must then be adjusted to reality, particularly given the limitations, both empirical and moral, on what may be achieved through the coercive power of the law. None of this changes, however, the standpoint from which political philosophy is to begin and from which it must judge these very concessions, namely the moral ideal of the good society. Political philosophy is thus understood as being at bottom applied moral philosophy.

On the contrary view, political philosophy should instead be understood as an autonomous discipline, setting out not from the truths of morality, but instead from the defining problems of the political realm, which are the exercise of power and the need for authority. People disagree and their disagreements extend from their material interests and desire for honor and status to their very ideas of the right and the good, so that society is possible only through the establishment of authoritative rules, binding on all and backed by the threat or use of force. As moral beings, we figure out how one ought to act, judge whether others have acted as they should, praise or blame them accordingly, and feel guilt or shame when we have ourselves acted wrongly. But as political beings, we must determine what kinds of action should be subject to coercion—that is, required or prohibited through the use or threat of force— and therefore what disagreements among us, not least those of a moral character having to do with what is right and wrong, should be settled in an enforceable way. Our focus must then be, not on how things ought ideally to be, but on how they can legitimately be made to be, given that people who must live together have opposing notions of the ideal. To be sure, political philosophy so conceived has a normative aim, seeking to lay out the basic principles by which society should be structured. But it carries out this project by asking in the first instance what principles, including principles of justice, ought to have the force of law. Though these principles may well be ones that can be established by purely moral reasoning, that is not in this context their justification. For political philosophy, their validity has to be judged by how successfully they handle the distinctive problems of the political realm, which are conflict, disagreement, power, and authority.

I mentioned at the outset what appears to be a rather empty definition of political philosophy: systematic reflection about the nature and purposes of political life. But perhaps it is not such a platitude after all. For the difference between the conceptions just outlined seems to turn on which of the two terms receives the greater weight. Should political philosophy look first and foremost to the purposes that ideally political association ought to pursue? Or should it set out instead from the nature, that is, the reality, of political association, which is that interests conflict, people disagree, and without the institution of law and the exercise of state power no common existence is likely to be possible? Depending on the point of departure adopted, political philosophy becomes a very different sort of undertaking. Either it forms a branch of moral philosophy, concerned with what ideally the good society should be like, or it operates by principles of its own, propelled in no small part by the fact that moral ideals themselves prove politically divisive. The difference, I insist again, is not that the second approach is any less normative by virtue of setting out from the permanent features of political life. For it understands these givens as constituting the problems that political philosophy must solve in order to establish how social life ought to be basically organized. However, the principles on which it must rely are held to be essentially political in character, defining the legitimate use of coercive power.

The contrast between these two conceptions is not unfamiliar. Sometimes philosophers endorse what is effectively the one and decry the other. Yet these professions of faith are seldom accompanied by much argumentation or by an attempt to analyze the supposed errors in the contrary view. Two recent exceptions have been G. A. Cohen and Bernard Williams, advocates of opposite sides in the debate, who expounded their positions at length (though without, unfortunately, ever mentioning the other). "We do not learn what justice fundamentally is," Cohen declared in explaining how he conceived of political philosophy, "by focusing on what it is permissible to coerce," for "justice transcends the facts of the world."[1] Williams, by contrast, maintained that "political philosophy is not just applied moral philosophy, which is what in our culture it is often taken to be.... Political philosophy must use distinctively political concepts, such as power, and its normative relative, legitimation."[2]

As I examine in this chapter and the next the nature of political philosophy, I will give particular attention to the pertinent views of these two philosophers. For they have brought out key features of the rival conceptions at issue—conceptions that Williams himself termed, rather to his own advantage, "moral-

1. G. A. Cohen, *Rescuing Justice and Equality* (Cambridge, MA: Harvard University Press, 2009), 148 and 291.

2. Bernard Williams, "From Freedom to Liberty: The Construction of a Political Value," in *In the Beginning Was the Deed* (Princeton, NJ: Princeton University Press, 2005), 77. In contrast to some of his other writings, Williams did not appear in his later political essays such as this one to intend any distinction between the "moral" and the "ethical," and I take this occasion to say that I myself use the two terms interchangeably throughout the present book.

ism" and "realism." No one has laid out so succinctly as Williams the substance of the realist position, even though there are many today, as I detail in the following chapter, who similarly invoke the name of "realism" in rejecting much of contemporary, particularly liberal, political philosophy as a flight from the reality of politics, which they regard as the omnipresence of conflict and the need for authority. (This view, rather than simply the idea that political philosophy should be modest and pursue realizable ideals, is, I should note, the core of what I too will mean by "political realism" in this book.) And though there are certainly other statements of the "moralist" or—more neutrally put—"ethics-centered" standpoint, the argument Cohen advances for his claim that the fundamental principles of political philosophy cannot depend on what it is permissible to coerce is of singular value. While it is aimed primarily at John Rawls's theory of justice, its significance is far broader: it shows what we would ultimately have to believe in order to reject as irrelevant the key considerations in favor of the realist outlook.

As the introduction has already indicated, my own sympathies lie more with this second, "realist" understanding. Political and moral philosophy ought to be seen as two very different enterprises in much the way it claims. However, I also believe that this, as it were, more political conception of political philosophy has to be formulated with greater care than it is usually accorded. For a crucial point to note is that Cohen and Williams like many others regard the choice between the two conceptions as stark and inescapable. Political philosophy, they presume, cannot in the end avoid taking one or the other of the two opposing paths. I think that this is a mistake. Political philosophy must indeed focus primarily on the characteristic problems of political life, which include widespread disagreement about morality, and for just that reason it demands a significant autonomy from moral philosophy. Yet it cannot determine how these problems are to be rightly settled except by reference to moral principles fixing the proper use of force and presumed to have a validity independent of the exercise of political power they serve to justify. There is thus a limit to the autonomy political philosophy can enjoy.

In the present chapter, I lay out the essential differences between these two rival conceptions of political philosophy and then explain—by a line of argument that is largely my own— why the realist view is closer to the truth. My aim here is principally critical, however. It is to show why it is wrong to regard political philosophy as applied moral philosophy. It should not, that is, proceed by way of elaborating a vision of how ideally society should be structured in order then to determine how this ideal can be accommodated to the realities of the political realm. These realities, the basic problems they give rise to and the sort of solution they require, constitute the correct starting point. Though I will of necessity have a certain amount to say about the alternative, "realist" conception, I have reserved to the subsequent chapter a more comprehensive treatment. There I will show how it should be better formulated than usual and thus in more detail how, in my view, the nature of political philosophy should properly be conceived.

2. Philosophy and History

In order to explain why political philosophy is not simply one province among many within the larger realm of moral philosophy, I must begin with some remarks about the nature of philosophy in general. I broach this topic with mixed feelings. Often definitions of philosophy come to little more than the expression of particular preoccupations and commitments, themselves disputable on philosophical grounds, but disguised as an impartial demarcation between what is "really" philosophy and what is not. Think of the idea that philosophy concerns itself with the conditions of possibility for experience, or that it consists in conceptual analysis. I am myself, to be sure, engaged in saying how one ought really to do political philosophy. Yet my intention is not to suggest that the positions I oppose fail to qualify as "philosophy," but instead that they fail to get it right about the "political." Still, the way I see the general goal and method of philosophical reflection plays a substantial role in the particular view of political philosophy I propose. That is why the following remarks are necessary, even if they perhaps also go to show that talk about the nature of philosophy inevitably ends up being philosophically controversial. I shall begin at least on neutral ground.

Philosophy, I believe, following Wilfrid Sellars, is the effort "to understand how things in the broadest possible sense of the term hang together in the broadest possible sense of the term."[3] It seeks to clarify the basic practices and goals inherent in our various ways of dealing with the world. Its ambition is therefore to be maximally reflective: philosophy differs from other kinds of inquiry in that it aims to spell out and critically evaluate the fundamental and often implicit assumptions on which they, as well as our experience as a whole, happen to rely. Even when it concentrates on some limited area, as in the philosophy of art or indeed in political philosophy, the concern is with the constitutive features of this particular domain.

This definition is, of course, extremely broad. It tells us little about the direction in which such reflection should go, and

3. Wilfrid Sellars, *Science, Perception, and Reality* (London: Routledge & Kegan Paul, 1963), 1.

different philosophers will proceed differently, in accord with their various views and interests. However, I want to mention one way the practice of philosophy cannot help but take on concrete form, since it forms an essential part of the justification I shall present of the proper task of political philosophy. It is a dimension whose significance philosophers themselves often overlook, so here I am clearly turning toward the philosophically controversial.

In striving to comprehend how things hang together, either overall or in some specific domain, philosophical reflection has to find some footing. It needs to draw upon existing knowledge and past experience, if it is to have any grasp of the problems it must handle and of the avenues it should pursue. The same point holds when the philosopher turns to challenge some widespread assumption, arguing that it is actually unfounded or less fruitful than commonly presumed. The resources for criticism have to come from what can count as settled about the matter under review. Philosophy is therefore always situated, shaped by its historical context, even as it aspires to make sense of some subject in as comprehensive, all-encompassing a way as possible. This historicity is easily discerned in the philosophical works of the past, and it inheres no less in the endeavors of the present, whether or not philosophers choose to acknowledge the fact. How could it be otherwise, given that reflection, however broad its scope, needs somewhere to stand if it is to see anything at all?

In this respect, then, philosophy is not so different from other kinds of inquiry. They too bear the mark of their time and place, both in the problems they tackle and in the solutions they devise. The modern natural sciences are no exception. Though they develop through the testing of hypotheses against evidence, hypotheses and evidence alike reflect the theories of the day, the experimental procedures available, and the course of previous inquiry.

Now just as a rootedness in history does not entail that the sciences fail to give us knowledge of nature as it really is, so it does not stand in the way of philosophy attaining a vantage point from which a deeper understanding of mind and world becomes possible. Some philosophers, it is true, have drawn such skeptical conclusions about both the sciences and philosophy itself. Some too have supposed that in order to be as reflective as possible, philosophy must stand back from the particularities of its place in history, in order to discover what Reason itself, addressing us simply as rational beings independent of historical context, requires us to think and do. These views, though frequently espoused, rest on a misconception. The contingencies of history are not essentially obstacles to be overcome, either in the sciences or in philosophy. They are the very means by which we learn about the world and ourselves as well as about how to learn about them, permitting beings like ourselves, who live in time, to lay hold of truth, which is necessarily timeless. Only through the accumulated experience of generations can we come to make out even the most basic features, not only of the world, but of human experience itself.[4]

Philosophy does differ from the sciences in its systematic devotion to examining the assumptions that implicitly shape our various activities, including the sciences and philosophical reflection itself. But this project does not demand setting aside what history has taught us about the matter under scrutiny—any more than the sciences are failing to progress when, relying on what they have come to know about their domain, they find

---

4. For a detailed defense of this position, see "History and Truth," chapter 1 in my book *The Autonomy of Morality* (Cambridge: Cambridge University Press, 2008).

themselves impelled, in their own "philosophical" moments, to reflect on basic assumptions they have tacitly been making. The effort to be maximally reflective does not involve detaching ourselves from the commitments that only our time and place have given us. Instead, it involves making the best use of the resources we happen to find at our disposal.

Now a consequence of these remarks about the nature of philosophy is that where we have learned through history to better understand the basic features of political life, political philosophy itself must change how it goes about its specific tasks. We can have reason to think that the way that political philosophy was practiced in the past is no longer justified, given what history has taught us about its subject. The import of this result will become clear as I go on, particularly in §§4 and 5 below, to set out how political philosophy in my view ought to proceed.

3. Two Pictures of Political Society

But first, another necessary preliminary. There have been, I observed, two competing conceptions of political philosophy. The one sees it as that part of moral philosophy whose aim is to lay out the principles of the ideal society, while the other regards it as centered on those enduring problems of the political realm—conflict and the need for authority—that stem not solely from divergent interests, but also from the right and the good being themselves a constant object of disagreement. I also suggested that fueling this dispute have been opposing ideas about whether the proper purposes or instead the actual nature of political life should provide the point of departure for philosophical reflection.

The latter remark, however, was a bit superficial, at best a first approximation to what is really at issue. For one thing, the nature of any human association, its typical activities and relationships, turns on the way it actually pursues some set of purposes. But in addition, we cannot determine the purposes it ought to pursue except by relying on some understanding of its nature. Without an idea of the aims and practices some association in fact embodies, we would not know the kind of association it is and would thus be in no position to pronounce on the purposes it ought to have. Unless you know what normally goes on in banks, you cannot say what a bank, as opposed to a supermarket, ought to do. Even when we are imagining an association that does not yet exist but would, we believe, serve to realize some desired end, we lean on assumptions about how it would function in practice. Otherwise, we would have no basis for thinking that it would be able to achieve the goals we want it to achieve.

All this goes to show that the conception of political philosophy as devoting itself to the moral ideal must still presuppose some picture of what political life is like, though this picture is bound to be very different from the one assumed by the rival conception. These two underlying pictures offer, in fact, a useful basis for tackling the theoretical debate that I have sketched. They serve to orient the different conceptions of political philosophy, and where they prove defective, doubts must also arise about those conceptions themselves. Moreover, they constitute in their own right another well-known opposition. Often they are identified simply by the names of the thinkers who have provided their canonical formulation. On the one hand there is the Aristotelian view of politics, and on the other the Hobbesian or Weberian view. The contrary associations such phrases easily evoke show how familiar this dispute too has become, and thus I can rehearse the main features of these two views of political society by reference to the figures I have just mentioned. (Needless to say, there are many important aspects of Aristotle's and Hobbes's political thought that, in focusing on this key contrast, I shall leave aside.) Though I believe the Hobbesian picture offers the truer account, it too has its shortcomings, so that neither of the rival conceptions of political philosophy is ultimately satisfactory.

According to the one view, then, political life is the highest, most comprehensive form of human association since its principal aim is to promote the ultimate end of all our endeavors, the human good itself. This is the position we encounter in the opening pages of Aristotle's *Politics*.[5] None of us, he remarks, can live well by living alone, for we have not the self-sufficiency of gods. Only in society are we able to obtain and make use of the means indispensable to a flourishing existence (*eudaimonia*)— not only the material resources needed to sustain our different activities, but also the education that enables us to grasp what flourishing consists in, as well as the public space in which to work out together how best to organize and pursue this collective enterprise. The various areas of social life, such as the family or the economy, are oriented toward attaining different parts of the human good. Political community is not simply one more kind of association alongside the rest, devoted to yet another particular goal. It encompasses all the others (*pasas periechousa tas allas*) as the most authoritative (*kuriotate*) kind of association, since its task is to ensure, through the just distribution of the necessary resources and opportunities, that our lives as a whole be the best of which we are capable. This su-

5. Aristotle, *Politics*, I.1–3.

premacy of political association comes to expression in the fact that the rules of justice it establishes (as opposed to those that may obtain within more limited social groups, such as the family) take the form of laws, coercively binding on all. However, the nature of justice, precisely because it bases itself on an understanding of the human good, represents a prior standard to which law, so far as given circumstances permit, aims to give institutional shape.

This is the picture of political society presupposed by those from Aristotle to the present who have held that political philosophy needs to proceed within the framework of the larger enterprise of moral philosophy.[6] I may have used some of Aristotle's own terms in describing this picture. But the idea that the function of political association is to establish the proper conditions for achieving together the sort of life it is best for us to live does not depend on the particularities of his philosophy, and it continues to possess a wide appeal.

Very different is the view of political society we find in the writings of Hobbes and Weber. I begin with Weber since his account provides the sharper contrast, rejecting all reference to ends and defining the political in terms of means alone. A group, he observes in *Wirtschaft und Gesellschaft*, may determine its membership either through voluntary agreement or by imposition, that is, by stipulating which individuals are subject to its rules independently of any consent on their part. Imposition (*Oktroyierung*) need not be by way of coercion. Some religious organizations (the Catholic Church, for instance) assert

6. At the beginning (I.2) and end (X.9) of the *Nicomachean Ethics*, Aristotle talks of ethics, the study of the human good, as being part of "political science," which is the "most authoritative and directive [*tes kuriotates kai malista architektonikes*] science" (1094a26–27). But by this he means that the latter studies the conditions under which the human good can be achieved.

authority over their flock from the very moment of birth even though, at least in the present day, their authority is solely spiritual and lacks the means of enforcement. But when, Weber adds, the group does impose its rules on individuals by the use or threat of force, it becomes a political association, and if it successfully upholds its claim to a monopoly on the legitimate use of force within a given territory, it acquires the particular form of a state.[7] There are different ways that states have sought to legitimate the power they exercise, including the appeal to ideals of the human good that they may purport to be advancing. But what makes them political in character and distinguishes them from other groups pursuing such ideals is the possession of the coercive means to implement whatever goals they happen to adopt.

Now Weber's focus on means to the exclusion of ends overdraws the difference between this view of the nature of political society and the Aristotelian view. In reality, if only implicitly, Weber is attributing to the state a particular end in portraying it as an association that claims a monopoly on the legitimate use of force. The fundamental business of politics, he is assuming, lies in the establishment of order, securing through the rule of law the conditions for civil peace and social cooperation. Nonetheless, this emendation scarcely narrows the gulf that separates the Weberian picture from the idea of political association as aiming essentially at justice and the human good. To the extent that these ends too may become the object of state action, the form they take, according to this picture, is determined by the primary political goal of creating and maintaining social order, through coercion if necessary. Justice as such cannot be the state's concern. It has to be justice insofar as it

7. Max Weber, *Wirtschaft und Gesellschaft* (Tübingen: Mohr, 1972), I.1.12–17.

forms part of an authoritative set of rules binding on all and serving in the first instance to replace conflict with cooperation. If this view of political society regards the establishment of order as the paramount end, the reason is not hard to divine. It sees the potential for conflict everywhere in social life: in the clash of interests, to be sure, but also in people's differing notions of the right and the good.

Such is, therefore, the idea of the political that animates the second conception of political philosophy. It should also be plain how widespread this idea is, and who its premier theorist has been. That is Hobbes, for whom the business of the state is, as he said, the "safety of the people," guaranteed by a "common power to keep them all in awe."[8] Hobbes's writings are unsurpassed, moreover, in the clarity with which they explicitly identify where these two pictures of political society differ. The ultimate point of contention, he explained, is the *kind of norms* that are most important in shaping its activities and institutions. The one view looks to *ethics*, the other to *law*. "It is characteristic of man," according to Aristotle, "that he alone, among living beings, has a grasp of good and evil, of the just and the unjust, and association based on these things makes a family and a state." To which Hobbes rejoined, "Where there is no common power, there is no law; where there is no law, no injustice."[9] For people, he insisted, tend naturally to disagree about what is good and evil—"there are as many different rules for virtue and vice as there are men" (*quot homines tot virtutis et vitii diversae regulae*)—so that law alone, as a body of enforceable

---

8. Thomas Hobbes, *Leviathan*, ed. Edwin Curley (Indianapolis: Hackett, 1994), introduction and I.xiii.8. (Throughout I will thus cite passages from the *Leviathan* by book, chapter, and paragraph number.)

9. Aristotle, *Politics*, 1253a15–20; and Hobbes, *Leviathan*, I.xiii.13.

rules binding on all, can provide a "common standard" (*communis mensura*) for living together, even as individuals continue (within the now instituted limits) to pursue their contrary conceptions of the human good.[10] These, I believe, are the different perceptions of its subject matter that steer political philosophy in the opposing directions we have distinguished: toward the pursuit of moral first principles or toward the need for order and authority.

4. Disagreement and Authority

Historically, the Hobbesian idea of political society has come to prominence in modern times, in reaction against the other, more idealized picture. So an important question is why this has been so. One sort of answer is very common. We meet it, for instance, in the essay that Leo Strauss published under the same title as this book, though the answer is not limited to the circles that tend his shade. The Hobbesian view has prevailed, Strauss claimed, because of a lowering of expectations and standards that is typical of modernity as a whole.[11] The aim has been to take a more realistic approach, to describe political life as engaged in replacing conflict with authority instead of fostering virtue and the good life, in order to ensure that it may more easily live up to its vocation.

No doubt this answer captures part of the truth. Yet it misses another motivation of enormous importance. I mean the recognition that the nature of virtue and the good life is a recurrent subject of disagreement and not solely as a result of inexperi-

10. Thomas Hobbes, *De homine*, XIII.8–9. See too *Leviathan*, IV.xlvi.32.
11. Leo Strauss, *What Is Political Philosophy?* (1959; repr., Chicago: University of Chicago Press, 1988), 40–55.

ence and error, but as the natural outcome of people reasoning freely and conscientiously about how one should live. The realization that moral disagreement is likely to be the outcome when reasonable people discuss among themselves the ultimate questions of life, or when a single person ponders them in her own mind, has been one of the seminal experiences of modernity. "By sowing questions and dividing them up," Montaigne wrote, "one makes the world flourish and teem with uncertainty and disputes.... *Difficultatem facit doctrina* [learning creates difficulty].... Never have two men judged similarly of the same thing, and it is impossible to find two opinions exactly similar, not only in different men, but in the same man at different times." Or as Hobbes himself declared (palpably echoing Montaigne), "Divers men differ not only in their judgment on the senses of what is pleasant, and unpleasant to the taste, smell, hearing, touch, and sight; but also of what is conformable to reason, in the actions of common life. Nay, the same man, in divers times, differs from himself, and one time praiseth, that is, calleth good, what another time he dispraiseth, and calleth evil."[12]

The important element in this outlook is not the mere idea that opinions vary. That people often disagree about ethical matters is a fact of life known from time immemorial. Aristotle himself began his *Nicomachean Ethics* with a survey of the rival notions of the good life (pleasure, honor, wealth, virtue, knowledge, and the various combinations of these). What Aristotle

12. Michel de Montaigne, *Essais*, III.13, ed. Villey (Paris: Presses Universitaires de France, 1999), 1067 ("En semant les questions et les retaillant, on faict fructifier et foisonner le monde en incertitude et en querelles.... *Difficultatem facit doctrina....* Jamais deux hommes ne jugerent pareillement de mesme chose, et est impossible de voir deux opinions semblables exactement, non seulement en divers hommes, mais en mesme homme à diverses heures"); and Hobbes, *Leviathan*, I.xv.40.

did not envision, however, but has become a leading theme in modern thought is that reasonable people, exercising their general capacities of reason on ethical questions as best they can and in good faith, tend to come to different conclusions—not through any defect of reason, but instead because of their different backgrounds, their different senses of what is salient, and their different ways of weighing disparate considerations. It is the realization that reason does not lead naturally to unanimity on these questions that represents the break with the past. Aristotle understood that political society must be organized so as to settle the various conflicts that inevitably arise among its members. Yet for him these conflicts were generally conflicts of interests, sometimes conflicts of opinions, but not conflicts in which reasonable people find themselves at odds about the nature of the right and the good. That is why he could so confidently look to ethics as the source of the principles of political community.[13]

Hobbes, by contrast, had a broader understanding of the sources of social conflict. Reason itself, he saw, can lead to contrary and competing views about the human good and social justice. This is why he and those following his lead have looked to law, not to ethics, as the foundation of political authority.

---

13. "Since in all arts and sciences," Aristotle declared, "the end in view is some good and the greatest good lies in the most sovereign [*kuriotate*] of all of them, which is the capacity for politics, the political good is justice, and it consists in what promotes the common interest" (*Politics*, III.12, 1282b14–18). He certainly recognized that people—in particular the wealthy few and the many—disagree about who should rule and about what justice means. But he did not acknowledge that justice could be the object of disagreement among people each having from their own perspective good or plausible reasons for their views. He regarded their reasons as being, from the standpoint of justice understood "absolutely" (*kuriōs, haplōs*), but "imperfect" or "limited" (*mechri tinos*). See on this score 1280a8–33 in III.9.

Later on in chapter 3, §2, when laying out the key elements of political liberalism, I provide a detailed analysis of the concept of reasonable disagreement. Here I will pause only to make a few clarificatory remarks about this concept. The first is to repeat a point I mentioned in the introduction. Though I regard the tendency to reasonable disagreement about ethical matters as an abiding theme of liberal thought and though I also consider it to be a central problem with which political philosophy must come to terms, I do not mean to suggest that liberalism is by definition, as it were, the only viable form of political philosophy. The idea is instead that an important way the liberal tradition, particularly in the form I call "political liberalism," differs from other forms of political thought is its keener sense of what are the essential problems of political life. It has grown out of an awareness of the failure of other, earlier political conceptions to fully acknowledge one of the chief sources of social conflict. This is, as I have said, the likelihood that reasonable people, exercising their general capacities of reason as best they can and in good faith on questions having to do with how the individual should live and how society should be organized, will arrive at opposing views. Whether liberalism itself can remain a viable idea in our world is a separate matter, about which I express some skepticism at the end of chapter 3.

This leads me to a second remark. The sense in which I use the term "reasonable"—in this chapter and throughout—is that implicit toward the end of the previous paragraph, namely, exercising one's general capacities of reason in good faith and to the best of one's ability. It should not be confused with other meanings the term has acquired, and in particular not with the way that John Rawls used the term when also discussing ethical disagreement and what he called the "burdens of reason."[14] By being reasonable he meant the willingness to seek fair terms of cooperation, in other words, a moral disposition that constitutes, he believed, the appropriate response to the problem that ethical disagreement poses for the organization of political society. In chapter 3, §2, I go through my reasons for not following Rawls's usage. But one reason should be readily apparent: the need to correctly characterize the problem itself.

The expectation that ethical questions are likely to be the object of reasonable disagreement is not, I should also caution, the same as the doctrine often called value pluralism, which holds that the ultimate sources of the good and the right, objectively speaking, are not one but many. Nor is it the same as skepticism, for which the proper response to intractable controversy is to suspend judgment or at least to regard one's own views as more an article of faith than a case of knowledge. Pluralism and skepticism are positions that arise in reaction to the pervasiveness of reasonable disagreement: their aim is, respectively, to explain or evaluate the phenomenon. Consequently, they too have formed prominent movements in the history of modern thought. And they have also not failed to become subjects of dispute in their turn.

The decisive fact, then, is reasonable disagreement itself, in all its breadth. For once it is recognized how pervasive such disagreement is, the idea that the aim of political association is to foster the good life of its members has to look out of touch with the reality of the human condition. Its central task, so the Hobbesian outlook insists, must instead be the construction of an authoritative order for the regulation of social conflict. No

---

14. John Rawls, *Political Liberalism* (New York: Columbia University Press, 1996), 48–58.

one, to be sure, would deny that adjudicating conflict is a political imperative. But in the Aristotelian picture, determining what each side is due takes place by reference to ideal principles of justice, drawn by moral reasoning from the character of the human good. The trouble is that the good and the right, human flourishing and justice itself, are notions about which reasonable people tend to disagree. Even should they deliberate on such a basis as carefully as they can in order to resolve the social conflicts that beset them, they are likely to end up simply adding to their number. The only effective way to settle social conflicts seems to lie instead in substituting for people's reliance on their moral convictions, with all their inevitable variability, the binding authority of laws, arrived at by legally established procedures. Naturally, the Hobbesian picture recognizes that material and status interests, too, can pit individuals and groups against one another and threaten the very fabric of society. But an appreciation of how deep and abiding moral disagreement can be, even among those who are reasoning well, constitutes its distinctive feature.

5. The Relative Autonomy of Political Philosophy

That I lean toward the Hobbesian picture should be obvious. Experience has taught us, I believe, that it offers a far more illuminating account of the nature of political society, not just in modern times, but throughout human history. We have learned to expect that in a free and open discussion reasonable people tend to disagree about justice and the human good—if not perhaps about simple points (the elementary rules of morality such as keeping one's promises and respecting the bodily integrity of others, and perhaps as well the importance of both agreeable experiences and actual achievement in a life lived well), then certainly about more complex questions as well as about the underlying principles that justify these judgments and explain the nature of the right and the good. The controversies about the makeup of human flourishing are notorious. But justice is no less contentious a subject. One need only recall the unending debates about whether individual desert, the general good, or the equal worth of each citizen should provide the basis for determining the proper distribution of material resources. Consensus on any of these subjects, when it occurs, is likely due to people failing to have thought deeply enough, to have listened to what others are actually saying, or to have escaped external pressures or internal inhibitions. Whatever unanimity premodern societies may have displayed, in their religious or ethical beliefs, largely arose from oppression or fear.

As a result, the corresponding "realist" conception of political philosophy, centered on the problems of conflict and authority, seems to me superior to any that regards it as principally engaged in mapping out the structure of the ideal society. Though Bernard Williams did not deploy the sort of argument I have been presenting, he could not have formulated the realist view better when he wrote that it identifies "the first political question in Hobbesian terms as the securing of order, protection, safety, trust, and the conditions of cooperation."[15] The sorts of moral ideals on which the rival, Aristotelian conception relies are bound to prove controversial. Being in themselves an important source of social discord, they form part of the problems of political life rather than their solution. For this reason, political philosophy cannot be simply one branch among others of moral philosophy. It has to be a more autono-

15. Williams, "Realism and Moralism in Political Theory," in *In the Beginning Was the Deed*, 3. See also "Human Rights and Relativism," 62, in the same volume.

mous and indeed more reflective sort of discipline, dealing with a domain shaped by the deep disagreements to which moral thinking itself so often leads.

This conclusion draws, of course, on an understanding of what we have learned through history about the nature of political society, about what it has become in modern times and about what, as we now see, it would have been all along, had there been the possibility of free and open discussion. However, as I was concerned to argue earlier (§2), there is nothing amiss in this way of proceeding. Philosophical reflection rightly makes use of the lessons of history. Some might see in such a stance the unwelcome implication that Aristotle's political philosophy is not really political philosophy. I prefer to put the idea by saying that, though his approach may have made sense in his day, it no longer represents, given what we now know, the route that political philosophy should take. Think, for instance, of what we would say about the practice of medicine before the discovery of the germ theory of disease.

Only up to a point, however, do I accept the Hobbesian picture of political society and the parallel, realist idea of political philosophy. For as I intimated earlier (§1), both are incomplete in a crucial regard. If political society rests on an authoritative order for the regulation of social conflict, what is it, we must ask, that makes such an order "authoritative"? The answer is that the order is authoritative if it generally commands the allegiance of the society's members, that is, if its various agencies of political rule are regarded by most people as entitled to settle as they do the conflicts falling within their jurisdiction. If most people instead comply with laws solely out of fear of the consequences of doing otherwise, without any belief that the state is entitled to impose them, the state may still survive, but it lacks authority. In order for a state to enjoy authority, people need not believe that every law it issues or every use it makes of the coercive power at its disposal is justified. What they must see as justified or legitimate is its wielding of power to establish the terms of their common existence.

Yet this leads to the further question of whether a political system can secure the perception of being legitimate without appealing to essentially moral principles explaining why it is entitled to impose its rules on the community, principles it must present as having a validity independent of the authority it possesses since they supposedly serve to justify its exercise of power and thus the authority it enjoys. As a rule, it cannot. The only exception is that, although states do need to put forward "legitimation stories" of just this kind, people may consider a state legitimate for different reasons of their own—be the reason simply that they see no better way available by which their common life can be secured. However, even then the account they tell themselves requires a moral foundation. For any conception of why a given state is legitimate must purport to answer three questions: (i) with what right the state may exercise coercive power, (ii) into what areas of social life it may justifiably extend its reach, and (iii) over which people it rightly has jurisdiction. In this respect, therefore, the Hobbesian picture is defective, and political philosophy, as it sets about exploring how political life ought to be organized, cannot ultimately avoid having to base itself on certain elements of morality.[16]

---

16. In Hobbes's own theory, this defect is obscured by his equation of morality, that is, "the laws of nature," with reasoning solely about what conduces to one's own advantage (see *De Cive*, II.1 and *Leviathan*, I.xv.41). For it is such reasoning, according to him, that moves us to seek civil peace and thus to adopt the necessary means thereto, which include bestowing coercive power on a sovereign. What Hobbes overlooked are the moral assumptions undergirding this line of argument. For instance, it embodies an instrumentalist conception of morality that rejects various

The import of the objection will be clearer if we attend to the difference between the concepts of authority, legitimacy, and justice. A state enjoys authority, as I use the term in contexts such as this, if it by and large commands allegiance to the laws it institutes.[17] Legitimacy, by contrast, consists in the state's entitlement to impose these laws on the people within its dominion. That is not the same as their generally regarding it as justified in exercising its power to institute laws, a circumstance that suffices to give the state authority but not, as we may say, legitimate authority. Frequently the two concepts are confused, as when legitimacy is equated with people's acceptance of the state's right to exercise the power it possesses. (I note some examples in the following chapter, which contains a more thorough discussion of legitimacy.) But that the two are distinct is evident from the fact that even when people believe a state to be legitimate and when a state claims legitimacy for itself, both are holding that this state's having the coercive power to secure the conditions of social order and cooperation really is justified, not merely that it is viewed as being so. Authority cannot be the same as legitimacy for the simple reason that it rests on a perception of legitimacy.

---

moral concerns, such as being impartial between the powerful and the weak and valuing right action for its own sake, that many would think essential (for some details, see *Autonomy of Morality*, chapter 5, §§2–3).

17. The term "authority" is used in several different senses. In my usage, it conforms to what may be called *de facto* authority, as opposed to authority in a *de jure* sense—the state's having the right to command the allegiance of those who are subject to it—which is equivalent to what I call "legitimate authority." In both cases, moreover, it is practical authority that is meant and not authority in the epistemic sense, as when we talk of the authority of experts, who have no right and are not perceived as having the right to expect that others will accept their opinions. For a helpful overview, see A. John Simmons, *Boundaries of Authority* (Oxford: Oxford University Press, 2016), chapter 1.

Because therefore the authority of the state depends on the widespread belief that it is entitled to exercise the coercive power it possesses, the legitimation story involved—whether valid or not—has to base itself on principles that are assumed to be binding independently of the state's authority. For they are being taken to justify that authority. They are, moreover, plainly principles of a moral character, as I have pointed out. We might go further and say that principles explaining with what right and in what respects a state may exercise coercive power over some particular group of people are principles of justice. After all, a regime that imposes its rule without possessing such a right is commonly said to be acting unjustly. However, the injustice involved does not belong to the sphere of distributive justice. Distinct from questions having to do with what is a fair distribution of the benefits and burdens of social cooperation, and indeed prior to such questions from a political point of view, is the question of the conditions under which any distributive scheme of basic rights and responsibilities may legitimately be instituted through state action. The question of just rule in this sense is the question of legitimate rule.

Legitimacy, then, is no more the same as justice than it is the same as authority. So much is already evident from the fact that the content of laws may be just without their having been legitimately enacted and legitimately enacted while failing to be just. But more fundamentally, a state itself may be a model of justice in the distribution of benefits and burdens it establishes, while being illegitimate in virtue of lacking the right to impose this scheme on some or all of the individuals in the society. Generally, for instance, it will have no legitimate claim on the allegiance of peoples it may choose to conquer, however just the structures of the society into which it forcibly incorporates them. Similarly, a state may be legitimate without being particularly just in its distribution of rights and resources. Even if it may be true that no state can be legitimate if too many of its laws are grossly unjust (though as I will also show in chapter 2, §7, legitimacy is properly a matter of degree), it is the conditions specifying when political rule may count as legitimate that determine how many is "too many." For there has never been a society in which some laws were not very unfair.

A good way to see the political priority of legitimacy to distributive justice is to note the following point. We all, it may be said, have a duty to support just institutions wherever they exist. Yet legitimacy, as I indicated in point (iii) above, involves a right on the part of a state to exercise its coercive power over a particular group of people, a right that entails a special obligation on their part to comply (other things being equal) with the laws it institutes, not insofar as these laws happen to be just and not merely because they fear the sanctions they may otherwise incur, but because the state is entitled to make laws to govern their conduct in particular.[18] Supposing (for the moment) that the American state exercises its rule legitimately, citizens of the United States would have reason in virtue of this fact alone to heed the laws it enacts.

As the preceding remarks make clear, the flaw I have pointed out in the realist understanding of political philosophy does not propel us back to the opposing, ethics-centered approach. The basic moral principles from which political philosophy must set out need not consist in some comprehensive vision of the human good. Nor, most importantly, need they derive from

---

18. In this regard, legitimacy involves what John Simmons has called a "particularity requirement." See his article "Justification and Legitimacy," *Ethics* 109, no. 4 (July 1999): 739–71, as well as *Boundaries of Authority*, chapter 3. I return to this aspect of legitimacy in the next chapter, §7.

justice understood as a moral ideal, that is, from a conception of
how society ought to be basically structured that is worked out
independently of the conditions under which its requirements
may be made legitimately binding on the society's members.
Rather, these principles must have as their primary object the
essentially political problem of determining the conditions
under which enforceable rules of social life may justifiably be
instituted, a problem all the more acute given widespread reasonable disagreement about what the ideal society would look
like. They can be said to involve an idea of justice in that they
determine the extent to which coercion, the use or threat of
force, may justly be employed. But they make the rest of justice, and so most significantly the principles of distributive
justice allocating the benefits and burdens of social life, subject
to the terms they lay down for becoming socially binding. They
thus form the foundation of what could be called *justice understood politically*—justice insofar as it may justifiably have the
force of law.

Though the conception of political philosophy I am presenting departs therefore from both the positions I began by
outlining, it remains far closer to the realist position. It can be
regarded as a more careful formulation of that view. For it remains committed to the axiom that political philosophy is not
applied moral philosophy, even if it also recognizes that political philosophy must anchor itself in principles of a moral character governing the legitimate use of coercion.[19] Suppose, for

19. Here and throughout this book I speak of justice insofar as it has some import for the organization of society, be it "justice understood as a moral ideal" or
"justice understood politically." Sometimes, however, we talk about justice in a more
expansive sense, as when we say that it is unfair that someone was not born in an
earlier age more suited to her talents, or died before he had time to demonstrate his
promise. Cosmic justice is not my topic.

example, that the state seeks to handle some urgent social conflict by instituting laws that happen to fit with the moral views of one of the parties involved. It has not then "applied" those views to the case at hand. Their adherents have already been doing that. The state has instead asserted its right to impose those views, by force if necessary. This is something different. It is claiming, not so much that the laws are morally correct (though that may be one of its reasons for establishing them) as that they are legitimately instituted. Political, as opposed to moral, matters have ultimately to do with power and its legitimate exercise.

Let me detail a bit further what this more complex conception involves. It does not, first of all, entail that spelling out the nature of justice as a moral ideal is a wrong-headed or futile enterprise. Describing what ideally should be each person's due, in advance of tackling the question of legitimate coercion, remains an important task of moral philosophy. The point is that political philosophy needs to proceed differently: any view of distributive justice it proposes should rest on an account of the conditions under which its demands may justifiably be made binding in a given society.

This requirement becomes particularly significant once we acknowledge, secondly, that reasonable people tend naturally to disagree about the right and the good. For we cannot then regard the conception of justice we ourselves may see most reason to endorse, when considering the matter in the abstract, as necessarily the one that ought to define the terms of our political existence with others. However convinced we ourselves may be of that conception's virtues, we have to reckon with the likelihood that other people, equally reasonable, will find it disputable. This is the inescapable reality of political life, and political philosophy must take its bearings from the basic facts of its domain. We need therefore an explanation of why our conception of social justice may justifiably be made a matter of law, an explanation that goes beyond saying simply that the conception is the one that reason recommends, since others, as we must recognize, can say the same about their own. If reason spoke with a single voice about which conception is correct, saying that might suffice (as it did, for instance, for Aristotle). But since the situation is otherwise, the conditions under which any scheme of social justice can be legitimately implemented take on independent weight. We may indeed continue to hold, despite the disagreement, that we have good reasons to think our conception is correct. (I show why this is so in chapter 3, §2.) But holding that our view is correct and claiming that it should be imposed on all are two separate matters, especially when the view is one about which reasonable people disagree. The principles defining the conditions under which the state may in general institute laws and thus exercise coercion constitute, as it were, "second-order" principles of justice, determining whether any particular view of justice may enjoy the force of law amid reasonable disagreement about what justice involves. In this regard, justice understood politically is inherently *reflexive*: it delimits what justice means, politically speaking, in light of the fact that the very nature of justice is so widely controversial.

A political conception of justice, I should emphasize thirdly, is by no means obliged to stop at the conditions under which people may legitimately be held to be bound by coercive rules making social cooperation possible. On the contrary. Political philosophy, properly conceived, may certainly go further and develop full-scale theories concerning the liberties, opportunities, and resources that citizens should enjoy. But such theories, if they are to remain essentially political in character, must regard the principles of distributive justice they propound as valid or correct only insofar as they satisfy the conditions of legitimacy. That is what makes these theories political theories of justice.

Finally, some words about what may appear to be a contradiction between two fundamental demands that political philosophy on my view must satisfy. On the one hand, it needs to take seriously the pervasiveness of reasonable disagreement about the right and the good, so that its primary concern must be the conditions under which authoritative rules for handling social conflicts may legitimately be imposed on the members of society. Yet on the other hand, as I have also argued, it needs to recognize that these conditions are essentially moral in character in that they concern the justifiable use of coercion. Can there not then be reasonable people who question or reject those very conditions?

Indeed there can be. But no contradiction is involved. The impression that one exists disappears once it is acknowledged that no political association, however legitimate, can be universally accommodating. Any conception of legitimacy, defining the extent to which coercive rules may be instituted for the sake of social order, cannot fail to entail the wrongness of some views about the human good or justice, even if there happen to be reasonable people—by which I mean (see §4 above) people exercising conscientiously their general capacities of reason—who happen to espouse them. There is no way to handle politically the problem of reasonable disagreement that is not itself, at least potentially, an object of reasonable disagreement. Principles of legitimacy have to be judged, not by their capacity to escape being controversial, but by the moral assumptions on which they rest. There has been a tendency, particularly in modern liberalism, to suppose it must be possible to devise a fully inclusive form of political association, one to which all those subject to it can see reason to subscribe, despite everything else that divides them. I explain in chapter 3, §4 why this sort of ultimate reconciliation of authority and liberty is an illusion. Every form of political rule excludes.

It may be objected that if this is so, if conceptions of legitimacy too tend to be the object of reasonable disagreement, there seems no reason why we may not, after all, seek to impose some scheme of social justice simply because it is in our view correct. That is what we must purportedly do with ideas of political legitimacy. The objection overlooks, however, the important difference between reasons to hold a view to be true and reasons to impose it on others, a difference that becomes all the more salient in the face of reasonable disagreement about the truth of the view in question. When we see good reasons to accept a conception of justice but others, from their point of view, see good reasons to disagree, it becomes obvious that reasons of a different sort, having to do with legitimate rule, need to be invoked if that conception is to be justifiably imposed on them nonetheless. In the case of principles of legitimacy, by contrast, the reasons to accept them just are reasons to impose them, legitimacy consisting in justifiable imposition.

Much more needs to be said about this conception of political philosophy. I need in particular to explain how it draws on ideas that, beginning with the late writings of Bernard Williams, have often gone under the name of "realism" and about how it also seeks to remedy their deficiencies. That is the subject of the following chapter. I want now, however, to step back and consider a fundamental challenge to my rejection of the ethics-centered view of political philosophy. It lies in G. A. Cohen's contention, fueling the critique of Rawls in his book *Rescuing Justice and Equality*, that principles of justice cannot in fact depend on the conditions of legitimate coercion. As I suggested earlier (§1), the argument Cohen presents for this claim is of far-reaching importance. If it is sound, then what I have adduced as the decisive reasons in favor of the realist position, even when it is modified as I have proposed, are not so at all, but in reality irrelevant.

6. Justice and the Human Condition

Let me quote Cohen's central claim again: "We do not learn what justice fundamentally is by focusing on what it is permissible to coerce." The coercive power of the state may well be needed, he concedes, to deter malefactors and to assure citizens of one another's compliance with the demands of justice in place.[20] But the conditions under which the state is entitled to exercise coercive power cannot delimit what justice itself is. The relation of dependence is the reverse. The conditions of legitimate coercion belong among the "rules of social regulation," rules he understands as devised on the basis of underlying normative principles, such as those of justice, and in the light of practical constraints in order to handle the various problems of social life—in this case, the need for enforceable compliance with the basic rules of society.

Now all these assertions are ones Cohen makes from what I have called the standpoint of moral philosophy. He is conceiving, that is, of justice as a body of principles that set out how society ought ideally to be structured and that are valid independently of any concern with whether they are to be made coercively binding, particularly in circumstances where people

20. The quoted sentence (Cohen, *Rescuing Justice and Equality*, 148) continues by explaining that "coercion is necessary only for deviance or assurance reasons."

are likely to disagree about their validity. But in addition, and most importantly, he is supposing that this is the standpoint that political philosophy should adopt.

At the very outset of this book Cohen says as much.[21] Political philosophy, he asserts, ought to proceed in the spirit of a "radical pluralism," drawing on the moral truth that there is an ultimate plurality of values—justice being but one among others—and that they are subject to compromises and trade-offs when we seek to realize them in our institutions and actions. This is the basis on which he holds that the principles to be made the object of state enforcement may have to depart in various ways from what justice ideally requires.[22] The basis is not, in other words, the reason I have given, namely that justice as it figures in political philosophy must be, not justice conceived simply as a moral ideal, but justice as subject to the conditions of legitimate coercion. Moreover, Cohen recognizes that the value pluralism on which he bases himself is a moral doctrine reasonable people can find controversial, for it represents a cardinal point on which he distinguishes himself from Rawls and many Rawlsians, who are his main adversaries in this book. Yet the fact that it can prove contentious is given no weight in the way he believes political philosophy should be pursued. He does not see in this fact or in reasonable disagreement generally about the nature of the right and the good any reason to think, as I have argued, that political philosophy should forego taking its point of departure in what happens to be one's own preferred moral philosophy, that it needs to practice a certain autonomy by beginning with the conditions under which the basic rules of social life can justifiably be made bind-

21. Ibid., 3–6.
22. Ibid., 286, 302–5.

ing. In his eyes, political philosophy is very much a matter of applied moral philosophy.

It might be thought that I am poorly placed to criticize Cohen on these grounds. Have I not myself claimed, in amending the "realist" view of political philosophy, that the conditions of legitimate coercion depend on principles of a moral character, principles that specify to what extent coercive force may justly be exercised in the establishment of social order? Is that not essentially Cohen's view as well? Yet these principles, so I have argued, need not be understood as deriving from a conception of the ideally just society that is defined in advance of any concern for how its requirements are to be made socially binding. That is how Cohen would understand them. But my point has been that the principles in question, responding as they do to the enduring political problem that conceptions of the ideal society tend to meet with reasonable disagreement, should be understood as serving to circumscribe the nature of justice *understood politically*—justice insofar as it can justifiably enjoy the force of law. These principles do embody an idea of justice in that they determine the extent to which the rules of social life may justly be made an object of enforcement. But they subordinate the rest of justice, and so the whole of distributive justice, to the demands of legitimacy they impose. There is therefore an important difference between Cohen's idea of political philosophy, which is a version of the ethics-centered approach, and the more politics-centered understanding I have been defending.

Nonetheless, I have yet to examine the fundamental argument by which he seeks to prove that the nature of justice cannot depend on what may be the conditions of legitimate coercion. This argument, developed at length in *Rescuing Justice and Equality*, is intended in fact to establish an even stronger conclusion. The nature of social justice, according to Cohen, does not depend on any sort of feature of the human condition. "Justice transcends the facts of the world."[23] No view could be more at odds with the conception of political philosophy I have been elaborating. For I have assumed, as no doubt many would, that the nature of justice in general, whether considered from the standpoint of moral or political philosophy, must reflect the basic facts about the human condition that make principles of justice necessary in the first place. That has been my premise as I have gone on to argue that we should include among these basic facts the tendency to reasonable disagreement about moral ideals, given how significant and abiding a source of social conflict historical experience has shown it to be. And this in turn is why I have contended that, if we then take the larger view and, instead of continuing to expound our own vision of the ideally just society, think *politically* about what society should be like in the light of deep moral disagreement, we will have to recognize that principles of distributive justice need to comply with prior principles—principles of legitimacy—setting out the conditions under which binding rules of social life may rightly be instituted. Yet this whole line of reasoning must be wrong from the start, if the nature of justice does not depend in any way on facts about human life and society. If so, it cannot be claimed that principles of justice should be subordinate to principles of legitimate coercion, which are manifestly not independent of such facts. Thus the serious challenge Cohen's argument poses.

I will examine this argument in two stages. First, I want to look at the way he distinguishes between principles of justice, which do not, he claims, depend on any facts about the human

23. Ibid., 291.

condition, and rules of social regulation, which do. The question here is not only whether this claim about the fact-transcendence of justice is plausible but also whether Cohen, in his own statements about distributive justice, is able to adhere to it. Then I will move on to the argument itself. It aims to show as a matter of logic that there must ultimately exist principles that are fact-independent and among which he places the basic principles of justice. Evaluating this argument will lead into a discussion of the very nature of normative principles.

I begin then with Cohen's cardinal distinction between "fundamental principles of justice" and "rules of social regulation."[24] The former define the ideally fair distribution of the essential benefits and burdens of social life without regard, he claims, to the question of how social life ought to be arranged in the light of any facts about human nature and people's beliefs and motivations. Rules of regulation, by contrast, are rules we devise on the basis of such facts as we apply fundamental principles of justice to the solution of various social problems. It is a mistake to confuse the two, as he charges Rawls with doing in having his theory of justice depend on the empirical factors he termed "the circumstances of justice"—limited scarcity, limited altruism, people's conflicting ends and purposes.[25] Such factors, which notably include what I have called the tendency to reasonable disagreement, are held to be relevant only for determining the rules of social regulation. That is why the conditions under which a conception of justice may legitimately be imposed can have nothing to do with the fundamental principles

---

24. Cohen's clearest statements of the distinction are to be found in *Rescuing Justice and Equality*, 269–71 and 276–79.

25. See John Rawls, *A Theory of Justice* (Cambridge, MA: Harvard University Press, 1971), 126–30; and Cohen, *Rescuing Justice and Equality*, 331–36. Though Rawls is his principal target, I come in for glancing criticism on this score at 148n65.

of justice themselves. While rules of social regulation are constructed in the light of practical constraints and typically imposed by legislation, principles of justice, he insists, are not constructed but instead grasped as holding true independently of any empirical facts.

Yet how solid is this dichotomy between fundamental principles of justice and rules of social regulation? Certainly, there are facts about what people want and believe on which it cannot be supposed that the nature of justice depends. No one should think that the fair distribution of resources has to respect some people's exceptional greed, their wish to be richer than their neighbors, or their prejudices with regard to various religious or ethnic groups. One may also wonder whether Rawls was right to let the terms of economic justice be shaped by the self-interest of the more talented and productive members of society, rewarding them (in accord with the "difference principle") with greater wealth so that they will have the incentive to engage in those activities whose effect is to make the least well off better off than they otherwise would be. This objection was the starting point of Cohen's critique of Rawls, and it has considerable force. But Cohen pushed his critique to the extreme. Can it really be true that the principles of justice, unlike rules of social regulation, are not grounded in any facts at all about the human condition?

Cohen declares that such is the nature of "that elusive virtue discussed for a few thousand years by philosophers who did not conceive themselves to be (primarily) legislators and who consequently had a different project."[26] Yet what illustrious phi-

---

26. Cohen, *Rescuing Justice and Equality*, 304. For the claim that principles of justice are completely "fact-independent," see 278, 285.

losophers of the past can he have had in mind? It is not surprising that someone like myself, given the political conception of justice I have proposed, should reject Cohen's way of contrasting principles of justice and rules of social regulation. But not even Aristotle, who likewise regarded justice as a purely moral ideal, would have endorsed it. He thought it laughable that the gods would care about justice ("making contracts and returning deposits") since they face none of the social problems that human beings do.[27] In one respect, Aristotle's position shares a significant element with my own: we both agree that the nature of justice cannot but reflect the basic kinds of empirical circumstances that make justice necessary. What drove him to a purely moral, insufficiently political, understanding of justice was his blindness to one such circumstance of key importance, the tendency of reasonable people to disagree about moral questions. Or to put the point another way: it is what historical experience has taught us about the prevalence of this phenomenon that recommends moving from Aristotle's conception of political philosophy to the one I am advocating. We can then see why justice, at least if it is, as I have said, understood politically, has to be understood with an eye to the need for authority and thus as having to start from the conditions of legitimate coercion.

I should, incidentally, point out that what I following others have been calling "circumstances of justice," though they include certain basic facts about the human condition such as limited altruism or reasonable disagreement, are not to be viewed as restricting what justice can require of individuals. Instead, they constitute the problem to which justice itself is a

27. Aristotle, *Nicomachean Ethics*, 1178b8–18.

response. What Cohen has at bottom lost sight of, I believe, is the important truth that normative principles in general are responses to problems.[28]

Now whatever the paucity of illustrious predecessors, the fact is that Cohen's dichotomy between principles of justice and rules of social regulation collapses in his own hands. Let me explain. At the heart of social justice, he claims, lies a principle of equality that "endorses deviations from equality if and only if the unequally placed parties are relevantly responsible for that deviation."[29] However, he is keen to add that justice also includes a "personal prerogative" entitling the individual to pursue his or her own interests to a certain extent. "Justice is fully served," he asserts, "only if people's access to desirable conditions of life is equal, within the constraint of a reasonable personal prerogative," since we have "the right to be something other than an engine for the welfare of other people: we are not nothing but slaves to social justice."[30]

Such remarks are certainly sensible. Yet note that Cohen conceives of this prerogative, whatever exactly its extent, as a

---

28. Thus, I agree with David Estlund ("Human Nature and the Limits (If Any) of Political Philosophy," *Philosophy and Public Affairs* 39, no. 3 [Summer 2011]: 207–37) that motivational inability does not as a rule block moral requirements, though unlike him I think this fact shows that "ought" implies "can" does not always hold. See my discussion in *Das Selbst in seinem Verhältnis zu sich und zu anderen* (Frankfurt: Klostermann, 2017), chapter 6, §4.

29. Cohen, *Rescuing Justice and Equality*, 310–11n51. This is Cohen's "luck-egalitarianism"; I take no stand here on its merits.

30. Ibid., 181 and 10. At 61, he says that only an "extreme moral rigorist" would deny such a prerogative, calling it again a "right." Much of Cohen's debate with his critics (see ibid., 373–411) revolves around the scope of this prerogative. What seems not to have been recognized is that to make it integral to justice as Cohen does undermines his dichotomy between fact-independent principles of justice and fact-dependent rules of social regulation.

"right" belonging to the very nature of justice, "fully served." It is not invoked as another kind of moral consideration that moderates the pursuit of justice. Rather, "justice is itself a compromise or balance between self-interest and the claims of equality."[31] Now what is this conviction that justice does not require that we become its slaves, if not an admission that justice would not *be* justice if its demands did not depend on certain basic facts about the human condition? Angels, from what I hear, are of a nature that would make them, unlike human beings, quite happy and fulfilled to be nothing other than engines for the welfare of others. We, by contrast, are divided beings, who in addition to being able to take up an impersonal standpoint have our own lives to live, with our own concerns and attachments. It is precisely the inescapability of this personal standpoint, and thus an empirical fact about the sort of beings we are, that Cohen regards as justifying the inclusion of a personal prerogative within the very nature of justice.[32] The laudable wish to avoid "moral rigorism" undermines his grand distinction between fundamental principles of justice and rules of social regulation.

Cohen, it should be noted, appears to suppose that principles, if they depend on empirical facts, must be ones we have devised or constructed ourselves, in order to solve the problems arising from those facts. Principles that are supposedly fact-independent, such as those constitutive of justice, are consequently to be understood, not as ones we construct, but as being true on their own. This is why he attacks the "constructivism" that Rawls espoused in his theory of justice (claiming its principles are those we would devise for ourselves in what

31. Ibid., 71.
32. This is the gist of the discussion in ibid., 9–10.

he called the "original position") and why he also holds that constructivism in general is an untenable view, since we can only set up new principles of conduct by basing ourselves on deeper principles we take to be antecedently true.[33] Now as I have myself argued elsewhere, and for the sort of reasons Cohen gives, constructivism is indeed an incoherent conception. Basic normative principles cannot be ones we construct or, as Kantians like to say, legislate for ourselves. They must instead be understood as principles we grasp or acknowledge as being true independently of any attitude we may take toward them.[34] However, it does not follow, as Cohen supposes, that they cannot depend on certain empirical facts. That supposition rests on a misunderstanding of the nature of normativity itself.

The misconception will become clear if we now finally look at his master argument for why there have to be fact-independent principles. This argument involves matters that are somewhat technical, demanding close analysis. But the effort will be worthwhile, as important truths are at stake.

7. The Nature of Principles

Cohen's argument goes as follows:

(1) Whenever a fact F confers support on a principle P, there is an explanation why F supports or represents a reason to endorse P.

(2) This explanation must invoke or imply a more ultimate principle, valid independently of F and able to explain why F supports P.

---

33. See not just ibid., 276–77, but chapter 7 in general.

34. See, for instance, *Autonomy of Morality*, chapters 4–5; and *Das Selbst in seinem Verhältnis zu sich und zu anderen*, chapter 4.

(3) The sequence cannot proceed without end because our resources of conviction are finite.

(4) Thus, there must be some ultimate, fact-independent principles.[35]

It should be plain that if this argument is sound, then political philosophy cannot, as I have maintained, take its fundamental bearings from such phenomena as the tendency to reasonable disagreement and the need for authoritative rules and legitimate coercion. But is it a good argument?

A first thing to observe is that this argument exhibits a well-worn pattern, and this alone should give us pause: A depends on B, but that dependence must depend on C, which dependence must in turn depend on D ... until we must come—for the regress cannot be infinite if it is to exist at all—to a prime mover, or to an ultimate fact-independent principle. However, I do not propose to dismiss Cohen's argument by means of guilt-by-association. Nor shall I plead that the regress can go on to infinity or resort to vague notions about justification needing no terminus since it is always a "holistic" affair of how a set of beliefs "cohere" together. My basis for rejecting this argument is a lot simpler.

First, consider what a principle is, in the sense under discussion. Principles are general rules of thought and action, asserting that certain lines of conduct are what we have reason to adopt in the sorts of circumstances they stipulate. Principles

---

35. Ibid., 236–37. I have followed his wording closely. It is important to see that Cohen intends this argument to focus on what is involved in a fact serving to *ground* or *support* a principle. That is not the same as the extent to which facts may determine the content or the range of applicability of a principle. Thomas Pogge's critique of Cohen ("Cohen to the Rescue!," *Ratio* 21, no. 4 [December 2008]: 454–75) seems to overlook this distinction.

refer to what we may call standing reasons for how to think or act: the principle that one ought to help anyone in distress is tantamount to the proposition that one has as a rule good reason to do so. Thus, the question of whether principles are grounded in facts comes down to the question of whether reasons are so grounded, and that means to the question of what a reason is. This question is notoriously a disputed area in philosophy, but here is how I see the matter.[36]

Reasons—by which I mean reasons themselves and not our beliefs about what reasons we have, as when we talk about "our reasons" for doing this or that—are both normative and relational in character. They consist in the way certain facts in the world *count in favor* (a normative relation) of certain possibilities of conduct, whether of thought or of action. The reason I have to carry an umbrella consists, not simply in the fact that it is raining, but in this fact counting in favor of the option of taking an umbrella. Reasons are called *prima facie* when they constitute presumptive demands that may upon reflection turn out not to have a claim on us and thus not really to be reasons. Usually reasons are *pro tanto*: though they truly apply to us, they may still be outweighed by what are on balance superior claims. Reasons count as *standing* reasons, however, when they are such as generally to override competing considerations. Yet in all these cases, reasons do not float free of the (nonnormative) facts, but depend, as I have noted, on the facts being as they are. So one wonders how there could be, as Cohen claims, such a thing as a fact-independent principle. Are not standing reasons precisely what principles of thought or action describe?

36. I present a more detailed account of the nature of reasons in *Autonomy of Morality*, chapter 5, §§6–7, as well as throughout *Das Selbst in seinem Verhältnis zu sich und zu anderen*. See also in this book chapter 3, §2.

True, sometimes certain facts count in favor of a line of conduct—that is, they give one reason to adopt it—only in virtue of a general principle that bestows on them that status. But this need not always be so. We can see a reason to take an umbrella some rainy day without relying on any general principle that makes it a reason, such as that one ought always to stay dry, since at other times we may not mind getting wet. Explaining why the present occasion is special may come to no more than detailing the various ways it differs from other rainy days (we are late for work, we are tired, the sky looks particularly dark, it has been raining for several days now, and so on). Though we would have to agree that, were another day to come along just like this one, we would also have a reason to take an umbrella, that acknowledgment does not express allegiance to some principle. One should not confuse the universality inherent in any reason as such with an underlying principle of the sort in question, namely with an explanatory principle. Every reason is universal, in the sense that it applies in a given situation only if it applies in all relevantly similar circumstances. Yet the general statement "in all situations of type S, one has reason to do A" is not a principle that explains why a particular situation of that type gives one the reason to act in the way indicated. It merely spells out what is involved in there being such a reason at all. A reason just is certain facts in the world (e.g., those having the features that make them of type S) counting in favor of certain of our possibilities (e.g., doing A).

Now if this is true of reasons, the same must hold for principles as well. Some principles may be grounded in certain facts because of underlying principles that make that so. But sometimes too, principles may be grounded in facts without there being any deeper principle that explains the grounding, if the standing reasons to which they refer have that sort of basis. In either case, principles are always grounded ultimately in facts, because reasons are so. Cohen, I suspect, believes otherwise because he supposes in general that the only way something nonnormative, the facts, can generate something normative, a reason or a principle, is through the intermediary of some further normative element.[37] But that supposition amounts to a misunderstanding of what normativity is. It is the way that nonnormative facts count in favor of possibilities of thought and action. If one finds that puzzling and thinks it stands in need of explanation, the source of puzzlement must really be the idea that there can exist such a thing as reasons at all. Reasons are by their very nature fact-dependent, so principles cannot be any different. For principles adduce standing reasons of thought or action, and these reasons are such as generally to outweigh contrary considerations because of the character of the facts on which they depend.

Thus, the principle "one ought not to cause pain" is grounded in what the very disagreeable experience of pain is like. We can say, if we like, that the principle would remain valid even if there were no beings capable of feeling pain. But all this would mean is that were any to exist, its ability to feel pain would give one reason to take the necessary precautions. There is a fact about what pain feels like if it happens to occur, and this fact grounds the principle that one ought not to cause pain. If pain did not feel the way it does (if, for instance, it never lasted long

37. That may well be because he also assumes that for one thing to ground another it must, in conjunction with other perhaps implicit premises, *entail* that conclusion. See David Miller's critique of Cohen's argument on this score in "Political Philosophy for Earthlings," in *Political Theory: Methods and Approaches*, ed. David Leopold and Marc Stears (Oxford: Oxford University Press, 2008), 29–48, esp. 31–38.

and was always immediately followed by a far greater feeling of pleasure), there might well be no such principle.[38]

It will not do to object that whenever a principle P is grounded in certain facts F, the statement "if any situation contains facts of type F, then one ought to act in accord with P"—or more succinctly "in situations of type F, one ought to act in accord with P"—will hold independently of there actually being any such facts F and therefore expresses a principle, call it P′, that is, to this extent at least, fact-independent.[39] For P′ is not a principle that *explains* why facts of sort F ground the principle P (which is what Cohen's argument requires). It is simply a statement to the effect that they do so. Moreover, the sense in which P′ is fact-independent is that there need not exist any facts of sort F for it to be true that, were they to exist, they would ground principle P. So this maneuver does nothing to disprove that principle P is ultimately grounded in certain facts of the sort F.

An example of an ultimate though fact-dependent principle may help to make my point clearer. Take the simple principle of prudence, which tells us (rather loosely formulated) to weigh together our long-term with our proximate good when deciding how to act. Counting in favor of this principle are the basic

38. Cohen suggests (*Rescuing Justice and Equality*, 245) that this very principle is fact-independent because its validity does not depend on the fact that sentient beings exist. He fails to consider the fact on which it is in reality grounded, namely the fact of what pain feels like.

39. Sometimes Cohen argues in this fashion, as when he declares that if the principle P_3, "we ought to express our respect for people," is grounded in the fact that "people possess what are thought to be respect-meriting characteristics," then that is only because of the "fact-free principle P_4" that "one ought to respect beings, human or otherwise, who have the relevant characteristics" (*Rescuing Justice and Equality*, 235).

facts of the human condition—that we are more than creatures of a moment, that life is full of unexpected changes, that present pleasure can lead to later pain. If it is now asked why these facts ground that principle, what is there to say? If it is insisted that they can do so only in virtue of some deeper principle, what could that principle be? That one should pursue one's good in a way that respects all the facts, both present and future? This is simply prudence all over again. No, either one sees, in the light of these facts, the standing reason to be prudent, or one does not. Nor should that be surprising if one remembers a general truth: reasons, being the way that facts count in favor of possibilities, cannot be such that, for the facts to count in that way, there must always be some deeper reason to explain why they do so.

What I reject, then, is the very first premise of Cohen's argument—that if a fact F supports a principle P, there must be an explanation why F provides a reason to endorse P. Rejecting the initial premise is, in general, the best way to handle regress arguments of this sort. To Aquinas's argument that there must be a prime mover since, whatever moves requiring a mover, the chain cannot go back to infinity, the proper response is to object at the outset, with Galileo at our side, "But it is just not true that whatever moves requires a mover." Similarly, it is not true that every principle-supporting fact or set of facts requires a further principle to make it one.

The facts therefore matter, even for philosophy. There is no way that political philosophy can determine what principles ought to govern our collective existence except with an eye to its basic and enduring realities. The challenge posed by Cohen's extreme version of the ethics-centered conception can count as dispelled.

Yet as I have also pointed out, political philosophy must look as well to principles of a moral character in determining how these givens of political life are fundamentally to be handled. In order to respond to the various sources of social conflict and to the need for binding and authoritative rules, it has to define the conditions for the just exercise of coercive power. This does not mean that political philosophy consists after all in the application of moral philosophy to the political world. For it must adopt a more reflective stance than is typical of moral philosophy. It needs to concern itself with how our common life should be authoritatively structured in light of the fact that moral philosophy, and moral thinking in general, so often proves controversial and divisive, even among the most reasonable people. Therein lies the autonomy of political philosophy. You have your moral views, I have mine, and each of us is convinced that they are right, standing ready to show the other the error of their ways. But once we confront the problem of how people like us are to live together, we enter the terrain of political philosophy.[40]

This understanding of political philosophy is therefore very different from both of the standard conceptions with which we began. Its difference from the ethics-centered approach should now be clear. But more needs to be said about how it differs from the "political realism" that is generally taken to be the significant rival. This is the task of the next chapter.

---

40. I hasten to add that this "autonomy" of political philosophy is a different matter than what I have called, in my book with that title (see footnote 4 in this chapter) the "autonomy of morality," the idea that the moral point of view only makes sense in its own terms.

2

The Truth in Political Realism

AS I HAVE observed, the idea of political philosophy presented in the previous chapter shares a lot with the conception, now often called "realist," that from Hobbes to the present has likewise opposed the ethics-centered approach. I too believe that political philosophy should takes its bearings from the fact that conflict is a deep and pervasive feature of social life. Even when people see the need to cooperate in order to achieve the ends they desire, they are likely to disagree about the terms under which their cooperation should take place—about who should fill what roles and about how much different persons should benefit or be burdened. Conflict and the need for settled rules to handle it are precisely what give rise to politics in the first place.[1] Moral reflection about the nature of the human good and the ideal society is not a suitable instrument for solving such problems, since these subjects are themselves among the enduring and fertile sources of disagreement, even among the most reasonable of people. Only the institution of some system

1. This, I remind the reader, is the core proposition of what is meant in this book by "political realism," and not simply the idea that political philosophy should be modest in its aims.

of authority—today the paradigm is the state—setting down with the means of coercion at its disposal what shall count as binding rules of social interaction can bring about the necessary degree of civil peace. Such, I agree, are the cardinal phenomena with which political philosophy must deal.

Yet I have also claimed that the realist view goes wrong in holding that the domain of the political should be understood without appeal to what are presumed to be antecedent moral truths. That cannot be done. A political order commands general allegiance only if those subject to its rule largely believe that it is entitled to exercise its power as it does. But they cannot thus regard this political order as justified except insofar as they believe it satisfies certain principles of an essentially moral character, principles that—as I specified in the previous chapter (§5)—identify (i) with what right it wields coercive power, (ii) in what areas of social life it may justifiably exercise it, and (iii) over what people it rightly has jurisdiction. Moreover, these principles, though not necessarily derived from some overall vision of the human good or the ideal society, must still be understood as having a validity independent of the authority of the regime itself. For they are being held to justify the coercive power it wields and thus the authority it enjoys.

Of course, people's beliefs about why their state is legitimate (if this is what they believe) are to a considerable extent the product of the state's own efforts to instill in them such beliefs. Given that a widespread perception of its legitimacy is the basis of the state's authority, it will naturally be keen to explain why it is justified in wielding the power it has and to use all the means at its disposal—schools, national holidays, constitutional documents, propaganda, religious institutions if they are under its control—to encourage acceptance of this account.

Still, the legitimation story the state promotes must have the structure I just described: to justify its rule, it has to refer to some account of why it is entitled to use coercive force as it does to assure the conditions of social cooperation, an account it must presume to be valid independently of the authority it possesses if it is to draw its legitimacy from that account. Different societies and different historical epochs will obviously have different understandings of what makes for political legitimacy. Consider, for instance, the two opposing pictures of political society I discussed in the previous chapter (§3). As long as the idea holds sway, as it generally has done in the past, that the principal aim of political rule is to promote the ultimate human good, legitimation stories are bound to appeal to what they take to be a people's highest ethical or religious ideals. Very different is the picture of political society that has arisen in modern times, that emphasizes the ubiquity of social conflict, particularly about ethical and religious matters, and that leads to legitimation stories that are correspondingly more limited and focused on the use of coercive power itself. But all these various understandings of legitimacy have in common that they regard it as rooted in antecedent principles of an essentially moral nature. This is why I suggested that political philosophy, though it ought to orient itself today around the second picture, needs nonetheless to pursue a middle way between the usual opposition between ethics-centered and realist conceptions.

In the present chapter, I develop this conception further. I do so in large part by examining more closely the leading form of political realism today. For even though its view of political philosophy seems to me importantly mistaken in the way I have outlined, I am far from rejecting it wholesale. On the contrary, I think it contains crucial truths that merit further elaboration.

My own conception of political philosophy should thereby take on sharper contours. I begin with some background, recounting how the political realism of recent years has grown out of a dissatisfaction with the main direction that political philosophy, under the influence of John Rawls's *A Theory of Justice* (1971), has taken in the Anglo-American world and how I have myself been led, by a different route, to a certain sympathy with this critique.

1. The Realist Revolt

The fundamental complaint driving this self-described "realist" revolt is that political philosophy has lost touch with the very nature of its subject matter.[2] In the effort to determine how society in the ideal should be organized, normative theorizing has become a means of escape from the realities of political life. The concern for consensus has obscured the permanence of conflict; the focus on questions of distributive justice has evaded the more basic fact that politics has to do essentially with the exercise of power. At issue is the broadly liberal framework within which political philosophy has come to be practiced—the primacy contemporary philosophers automatically accord to individual freedom, equality, and social welfare. The point is not so much that liberalism itself should be rejected or those values demoted as that political philosophy needs to be able to stand back from the reigning ideas of the day and see liberalism from the outside, as one political conception among

---

2. William Galston's essay, "Realism in Political Theory," *European Journal of Political Theory* 9, no. 4 (October 2010): 385–411, is still a helpful survey of this development. But see too the more recent book by Matt Sleat, *Liberal Realism* (Manchester: Manchester University Press, 2013).

others, one that like them is historically conditioned, sincerely contested by many, and inescapably (if not always explicitly) committed to establishing mechanisms of rule that exclude its enemies and shape the thinking of the rest of society.

Political philosophy, it is charged, has become insufficiently political. It has turned into a branch of ethics, drawing up blueprints of the ideal society that everyone should supposedly be able to see reason to endorse. The situation has not significantly changed, many feel, with the more political emphasis of the later Rawls. For though his "political liberalism" does eschew comprehensive conceptions of the human good as too controversial to serve anymore as the foundation of political philosophy, it still aims primarily at a conception of distributive justice—or more exactly a "family" of liberal conceptions of justice—it presumes can be the object of a "reasonable overlapping consensus."[3] Yet the nature of justice is no less controversial than other ethical matters. Political philosophy ought to regard as its starting point the ubiquity of conflict and thus the necessity of state power to create the conditions of social order.

The dissenting voices I have evoked do not form a single movement. Their call for political philosophy to recover a sense of the real nature of politics occurs as part of widely different theoretical programs. However, one figure stands out because of the particularly probing way in which he developed this common theme. That figure is Bernard Williams, who in a number of mostly posthumous essays argued that political philosophy has lapsed into "applied moral philosophy," taking its cue from "a morality prior to politics," and that it should instead recognize conflict and power as the defining political phenomena

---

3. John Rawls, *Political Liberalism* (New York: Columbia University Press, 1996), xlv–xlvi.

and therefore legitimacy—that is, the legitimate use of force—
rather than distributive justice as the primary normative concept with which it must deal.[4] These views Williams intended
to elaborate in a book about politics he was writing at the time
of his death but sadly never completed. Nonetheless, the account the essays provide is rich and provocative enough to
serve in many respects as a canonical statement of the reso-
lutely political conception of political philosophy I have been
describing. As I go on to investigate this conception further, I
will take as a benchmark the views Williams outlined, following him in, among other things, giving it the name of "political
realism."[5]

As I have mentioned, I am, moreover, in considerable agreement with the understanding of political philosophy he was ar-
ticulating. I too have argued that the principal aim of political
philosophy cannot be to work out a theory of the ideal society,
since the major sorts of social conflict it must address arise, not

4. Bernard Williams, *In the Beginning Was the Deed* (Princeton, NJ: Princeton
University Press, 2005), 2, 3, 5, 7, 77. As I noted in the preceding chapter, Williams
did not in these political writings, as in some of his earlier writings, use the term
"moral" as a contrast with "ethical" or associate "morality" with a Kantian conception. I follow suit.

5. I might also have taken as representative some of the writings of Raymond
Geuss, whose conception of political realism overlaps with that of Williams. However, I have decided to leave them aside since they are marred by historical dis-
tortions, such as the notion that liberalism is "the attempt always to see society
sub specie consensus" (*History and Illusion in Politics* [Cambridge: Cambridge University Press, 2001], 4)—for the one-sidedness of this view, see my remarks in the
introduction—as well as by the silly if not irresponsible idea of enrolling political
realism under the banner of a "neo-Leninism" (*Philosophy and Real Politics* [Prince-
ton, NJ: Princeton University Press, 2008], 23–30, 99). Furthermore, Geuss's political realism consists largely in criticizing the views of others without ever making
clear the normative assumptions on which he himself relies. In this sort of evasive-
ness he follows his philosophical model, Adorno.

only from people's passions and interests, but also from their convictions about the good and the right, which are likely to diverge even when they are reasoning conscientiously. That is why, given the deep disagreements to which moral thinking so often leads, political philosophy cannot consist in anything like applied moral philosophy. It has to be a more autonomous sort of enterprise. As I put the point near the end of the previous chapter,

> You have your moral views, I have mine, and each of us is convinced that they are right, standing ready to show the other the errors of their ways. But once we confront the problem of how people like us are to live together, we enter the terrain of political philosophy.

Thomas Hobbes expressed a similar view:

> When men that think themselves wiser than all others clamor and demand right reason for judge, yet seek no more but that things should be determined by no other men's reason but their own, it is as intolerable in the society of men as it is in play, after trump is turned, to use for trump on every occasion that suit whereof they have most in their hand.[6]

Like Hobbes, I believe that political philosophy has its own agenda. It must deal in the first instance with the problems of authority and legitimacy, with the reasons people can see to subordinate their individual purposes to a common power and with the conditions under which the exercise of that power is justified or legitimate.

---

6. Thomas Hobbes, *Leviathan*, ed. Edwin Curley (Indianapolis: Hackett, 1994), I.v.3.

Rawls too, it should be noted, declared that political philosophy is not "applied moral philosophy."[7] However, what he meant falls short of the crucial point. His idea was that political philosophy should not consist in applying to the political domain some comprehensive religious, moral, or philosophical doctrine about the ultimate ends of man, but should focus instead, as does his own "political liberalism," on the essential structure of political association—namely, the principles, essentially coercive in character, that govern the way a society's main institutions fit together into one system of social cooperation—in order to ask which such principles would constitute fair terms of cooperation. This line of thought is on the right track. But it does not go far enough. It skirts the fact that people disagree, even when reasoning to the best of their abilities, about what fair terms of cooperation would be. That is why political philosophy must concern itself first of all with the question of authority and legitimacy.[8]

I have come to these realist conclusions by a different route than Williams, namely through reflecting on the moral presuppositions of political liberalism itself. It will be useful if I summarize at the outset the path my thinking has taken. (A more systematic account appears in the following chapter.) The central goal of political liberalism, as Rawls, I, and others have conceived it, is to reformulate the core principles of liberal democracy without appeal to the individualist philosophies that

7. John Rawls, *Justice as Fairness: A Restatement* (Cambridge, MA: Harvard University Press, 2001), 14; also 181–82.

8. In his later period of *Political Liberalism*, Rawls did turn his attention to the concept of political legitimacy (see the next chapter), a concept that receives no mention in *A Theory of Justice*. However, he appears not to have realized that this concept must take priority over that of justice.

shaped the classical liberalism of such figures as Locke, Kant, and Mill. As shown by its devotion to the ideal of toleration, liberalism has always been a response to the breadth of social disagreement, seeking terms of political association to which people can agree despite all that divides them. Political liberalism aims to carry this concern further. Especially in the wake of the Romantic rediscovery of the importance of tradition and belonging, the individualist values of thinking for oneself and working out on one's own how one will live—however influential in modern society—have themselves become, no less than religious creeds or other ideas of the human good, objects of controversy about which reasonable people are likely to disagree.[9] The basic principles of political association, it is argued, need to prescind from such views as well as from all comprehensive ethical doctrines.

Yet if liberalism, now understood as a strictly political conception, is to be "freestanding" in this way, it cannot stand free from moral assumptions altogether. Otherwise, one cannot explain why liberal thought ought to abandon its past dependence on individualist ideals. I have sought to bring out more clearly than Rawls himself what these key assumptions are. The most important is the conviction that, because political principles differ from other moral principles in being coercive in nature, backed by the use and threat of force, people ought not to be held to be subject to them unless they can also endorse the reasons for imposing them. Only so will they then be treated not merely as means, their compliance to be enforced for the

9. I must signal, once again, that by "reasonable" I mean here and elsewhere exercising one's general capacities of reason to the best of one's abilities. This is a broad epistemic notion and therefore distinct from the moral sense of "reasonable"—being disposed to seek fair terms of cooperation—that Rawls and others have deployed. For further discussion, see §2 of the next chapter.

sake of social order, but also as persons in their own right, as beings who do not simply (as the higher animals can as well) think and act on the basis of reasons but can also determine by reflection which reasons they ought to guide themselves by. It is this specific conception of respect for persons (to be distinguished from the many other things the notion of respect has been taken to mean) that forms the core of the liberal idea of political legitimacy. That idea, as I now formulate it more carefully, is the requirement that the fundamental principles of political society, being coercive in nature, should be such that all who are subject to them must be able from their perspective to see reason to endorse them, assuming a commitment—which some may in fact not have—to this principle of respect, that is, to basing political association on principles that can meet with the reasonable agreement of its citizens.[10]

However, this principle of respect is one that some people have from their standpoint good grounds to reject. They may be of the view, for instance, that the crucial feature of political principles is that they be pleasing to God, whether they happen to accord or not with the reason of those whom they are to bind. Liberalism, for all its desire to be inclusive, also excludes, as every political conception does. I shall have more to say about this fact toward the end of this chapter (§8) and in the next (§4). Here my aim has been to explain why I have come to an appreciation of many of the central ideas of political realism,

---

10. For more on this principle of respect and the idea of legitimacy it entails, see the following chapter, §§3–4. There I show, among other things, how this principle underlies, for instance, what Rawls called "the liberal principle of legitimacy": "Our exercise of political power is proper and hence justifiable, only when it is exercised in accordance with a constitution the essentials of which all citizens may be reasonably expected to endorse in the light of principles and ideals acceptable to them as reasonable and rational." See his *Political Liberalism*, 217; also 137.

including with regard to the present point. Conflicts in moral belief among reasonable people are endemic in social life, and to an extent that liberal thought itself has often underestimated. Political philosophy loses sight of this fundamental truth about politics when it supposes its primary object consists in determining how a just society ought ideally to be organized. People differ deeply about what justice means and entails. Political philosophy needs therefore to deal first of all with the question of how social order is possible and thus with how the state ought to exercise its power to bring it about.

Realism in the form that Williams expounded seems to me nonetheless flawed. My chief disagreement has to do with his claim that political philosophy ought to avoid appealing to "a morality prior to politics." As I have already indicated, I do not think this is possible, even when the focus is the distinctively political question of the conditions under which the exercise of state power is legitimate. Later in this chapter I go much further into my reasons for rejecting his view. First, however, I want to lay out less autobiographically and more systematically what I find correct in the general orientation of political realism.

2. The First Political Question

A good point of departure is another of John Rawls's fundamental assumptions, one that was integral to his understanding of political philosophy itself. Near the beginning of *A Theory of Justice*, he declared,

> Justice is the first virtue of social institutions, as truth is of systems of thought. A theory however elegant and economical must be rejected or revised if it is untrue; likewise laws and institutions no matter how efficient and well-arranged must be reformed or abolished if they are unjust.

Rawls returned to this view at the end of his book, saying that it expresses "a common sense conviction."[11] Yet the idea that justice (he meant distributive justice) is the first virtue of social institutions is not the truism it may appear to be. To be sure, social institutions that are unjust are importantly defective, and steps should be taken, if possible, to bring the society closer to what justice requires. But should the reform or abolition of unjust institutions take precedence over every other sort of consideration? Should these goals be pursued at the expense of whatever other merits the institutions may possess? This is apparently what Rawls meant when he attributed to justice the status of a first virtue. "An injustice is tolerable," he explained, "only when it is necessary to avoid an even greater injustice."[12] The fact that certain institutions are unjust gives us supposedly sufficient reason either to correct them or to abolish them, "no matter how efficient and well-arranged" they may be, so long as justice would not elsewhere be compromised even more. But is this true? Can it really be maintained that justice is in this sense the first virtue of social institutions?

Consider Rawls's own statement that "a society is a cooperative venture for mutual advantage."[13] As a definition, this will hardly do, since society is not itself a venture but consists in the shared habits of thought and action that, making us who we are, enable us to undertake the various ventures we pursue.[14]

11. John Rawls, *A Theory of Justice* (Cambridge, MA: Harvard University Press, 1971), 3, 586. Rawls, one should note, added (3) that this thought may be "expressed too strongly."

12. Ibid., 4.

13. Ibid.

14. One might also object that people are members of society—and therefore subjects of distributive justice—even when they are too old or disabled to enter into cooperative relations. On this point, see Martha Nussbaum, *Frontiers of Justice* (Cambridge, MA: Harvard University Press, 2006).

However, the idea Rawls had in mind is that the justice (the distributive justice) of a society's institutions has to do with the terms on which they enable cooperation among its members. Although people count as cooperating if they are acting together so as to produce results that are to the advantage of them all (relative to the absence of cooperation), the rules by which they cooperate are unjust if some profit more from the results than they should and others less, because for instance the rules have been dictated by differences in power among the parties concerned. Relations of mutual advantage are just only if they are fair.

Now precisely because unjust institutions may still be mutually beneficial, reforming or abolishing them simply because they are unjust, without attending to any other considerations, can sometimes mean a loss in social cooperation. Perhaps if such an institution is eliminated, no other way of coordinating people's actions in this area of social life will then be possible. Or perhaps making the rules of the institution more just will lead those who profited from the previous arrangement to no longer take part in the institution's activities. Not in every case, to be sure, does cooperation serve to achieve some actual good (a gang of thieves can work together), but when it does, it may do so without its terms being just (a factory can make a useful product even though its workers are exploited). For that reason, the pursuit of justice sometimes needs to be weighed against the importance of there being cooperation at all. Depending on the circumstances, justice may not always prove to be the first or overriding virtue of social institutions.

The situation is not in fact so different with truth and systems of thought. All else being equal, Rawls is right: "a theory however elegant and economical must be rejected or revised if it is untrue." But it can sometimes be better to hold on to an overall view of things we know to be in certain respects false or only approximately true, if the alternative is to have no comprehensive view at all or one whose scope has been reduced to the parts that are strictly true. For without such a view, we may lack the ability to orient ourselves in the world, to make sense, if only partially, of the things that interest us. Truth is certainly the *supreme* virtue of systems of thought, as justice is of social institutions: they are what we ultimately aim at. But they are not necessarily the *first* virtue, the value whose pursuit must always outweigh other considerations.

Social institutions can thus embody valuable forms of cooperation, however just or unjust their defining rules may happen to be. Their existence depends, however, not merely on the rules, but also on people feeling they have the reasonable expectation that if they do their part and comply with the rules, others will do so too. Moreover, a society's institutions do not simply coexist. They interact, sometimes coming into conflict, but more often—if the society is to hold together—relying on one another in order to function as they do. A society is a system of forms of cooperation. In order to ensure that its different institutions cohere in this way and to provide in general the conditions of security and trust without which all cooperation would be narrow and episodic, a society must introduce laws. That means, it must organize itself politically, giving itself some form of government to widen and strengthen the conditions for social cooperation.

Political rule of some sort is therefore indispensable. At certain times and to a limited extent, elementary forms of social cooperation may develop spontaneously. People may see that if they each do their part in some common activity provided that others do so as well, they will achieve some mutual benefit, as in Hume's famous example of two persons in a rowboat who begin, without any explicit agreement, to row in synchrony because otherwise they cannot move at all.[15] However, people's passions can get in the way of their reasoning. They can also be divided in their interests. They may furthermore have different conceptions of the human good and of what is right and fair. Perhaps one of the rowers desires the glory of being the commander, or the rowers disagree about their destination. They may also differ about whether rowing is a sport or just a means of transportation, as well as about when it is appropriate to take a rest or about who should do the steering.

Of course, rowboating is generally a simple affair, untroubled by such concerns. But not so the more complex and consequential kinds of cooperation on which societies depend. Despite the necessity for people to work together if they are to survive and flourish as a community, their passions, interests, and views about the good and the right often put them at odds, particularly when matters of importance are at stake. Social disorder and breakdown can ensue. The need for cooperation and the basic human tendencies that render it difficult if not impossible form, we may say, *the circumstances of politics*.[16] They constitute the problem to which political rule is the solution. For only if people see their conduct as subject to authoritative rules, that is, to rules or laws imposed by a system of government they regard as having a claim on their allegiance, will they be able to cooperate with one another on a broad and consistent basis. It ought not to be thought that the problem of order belongs to the past, that at least in the rich Western democracies the conditions of social cooperation are now secure, unimperiled by

15. David Hume, *A Treatise of Human Nature* (Oxford: Clarendon, 1975), 490.

16. Cf. the similar conception in Jeremy Waldron, *Law and Disagreement* (Oxford: Oxford University Press, 1999), 102–6.

the conflicts that remain. The events of 1920s and '30s, if not the '60s as well, should remind us that the problem of social order is never solved once and for all. Today political violence in the West is unmistakably on the rise, and whether states can continue to secure the conditions of social cooperation as the effects of global warming, for instance, become more palpable is very much an open question.

Now although in general not all forms of political rule can properly be called states, having definite territorial boundaries, a centralized administration, and codified procedures for the enactment of laws, I will henceforth speak only of states, since they are the characteristic mode of rule in modern times. Typically, the state claims that the laws or rules of cooperation it institutes are just or that it has tried to make them so. But its first task must be to guarantee the possibility of social cooperation itself, and that means setting up rules that, whatever their actual justice, will be authoritative. For the nature of justice and its demands in specific situations are subjects about which people differ, and their differences can run so deep as to keep them from joining together in common endeavors. As a number of early modern thinkers recognized (I already cited Hobbes on this score), individuals reasoning about what is good and right are likely to disagree, so that the primary purpose of the state must be, not the realization of justice, but rather the establishment of order. For social cooperation of any significant sort to be possible, people must have the assurance that all will comply with the same set of rules determining, be it justly or not, what they own, what they may do with what they own, and how they may and must act in regard to one another. Often being perceived to be, if not just, then not too unjust may be necessary for the rules to have authority, that is, for them to be rules people believe they should obey. But the main thing is that the state, with the coercive means at its disposal, make the rules both binding and authoritative.

Thus Bernard Williams was right to assert, in the cardinal axiom of his political realism, that "the first political question" is

> the securing of order, protection, safety, trust, and the conditions of cooperation. It is "first" because solving it is the condition of solving, indeed posing, any others. It is not (unhappily) first in the sense that once solved, it never has to be solved again.[17]

The securing of social order must be the state's first business, since every other undertaking presupposes that social order has been achieved and continues to be maintained. With this part of Williams's political realism I could not agree more.

3. The Concept of Legitimacy

The state can ensure the conditions for social cooperation only if, as I have said, the rules it seeks to impose are authoritative. By and large people must believe they have good reason to comply with them, even if their passions and interests or their own ideas of what is good and right may move them to wish that society were organized differently. Obviously, the state's possession of means of enforcement figures among the reasons for compliance: a state cannot enjoy authority if it is seen to lack the power to handle the conflicts that imperil social cooperation. ("Failed states" are the extreme example.) But threats and coercion alone cannot suffice to give the state authority. By themselves, they would make the law the state imposes sim-

17. Williams, *In the Beginning Was the Deed*, 3; also 62. Subsequent references to this book will be given in the text, preceded by the abbreviation IBD.

ply a set of commands that people are bullied into obeying, without any sense that they are obligated to obey it. No doubt some persons do look at the law in this alienated way. But most people—or most people with any power or resources—cannot do so without the forms of cooperation that result being stunted and fragile. For social cooperation to flourish, laws must be authoritative. People in the society must largely believe that the state has a claim on their allegiance, that it is—to some extent anyway—*entitled* to impose these rules on their conduct. In other words, they must consider the state to be (to this extent) *legitimate*, justified in its use of coercive power to institute the rules of their social life.

Consequently, if the state is to accomplish its task of making social cooperation possible, it must seek to legitimate the legislative and administrative power it exercises. It must, as in fact every state does, develop some legitimation story—claiming for instance that it derives from some mythical founding, that the monarch is God's representative on earth, that all its citizens have consented to its institution or have from their different perspectives good reason to do so, that the leader is the voice of the people—that explains why it is entitled to rule.[18] This is so even if, as I remarked before (chapter 1, §5), people may sometimes regard a state as legitimate for reasons quite different from those the state asserts, considering perhaps its rule as justified simply because it appears to them the least of the possible evils. Be this as it may, the hallmark of any political order, Max Weber rightly held, is that it seeks to secure obedience to

18. Of course, some political regimes, instead of seeking to contain social conflicts, have fomented them, denouncing some minority as the enemy of the rest of society and thus making it part of their legitimation story that they alone are able to protect the social fabric from this supposed internal threat.

its rules by what it claims to be the legitimate use or threat of force.[19] Indeed, as Weber also observed, those who hold political power are in this regard like anyone who possesses some significant social advantage: they feel obliged to have on offer for others who are less well situated (and may challenge their superior position) some account of why they are justified in possessing it.[20]

Because, moreover, the nature of the good and the right have come to appear eminently controversial, even among reasonable people, I have argued that political philosophy itself should now see its primary (though naturally not exclusive) concern to lie with the idea of legitimacy rather than, as so often, with that of distributive justice. In the preceding chapter (§5), I offered an initial clarification of this concept. The legitimacy of a system of political rule, I pointed out, has three aspects: it consists in the state having the right to exercise coercive power in certain specific regards over a group of people rightly considered to be within its jurisdiction. However, my chief aim then was to point out that legitimacy and authority are quite distinct notions, and it will be useful to develop this point a bit more before going deeper into the nature of legitimacy itself.

Sometimes philosophers and social scientists effectively equate these two concepts, employing a subjective notion of legitimacy that identifies it with the fact that people generally believe the state to be entitled to exercise its coercive power over them. As I indicated, this usage is ill-conceived. A state is legitimate if it is actually justified in its wielding of coercive power. (Since it may be more or less justified in this regard, legitimacy is properly speaking a matter of degree—a point that

19. Max Weber, *Wirtschaft und Gesellschaft* (Tübingen: Mohr, 1972), I.1.17.
20. Ibid., II.9.3.

will prove important toward the end of this chapter.) That is after all what the term means. For when people do accept a state as justified in its rule, that is, as legitimate, and when a state claims legitimacy for itself, they are holding that the state's exercise of power really is legitimate or justified and not merely, indeed tautologously, that they believe it to be so. Legitimacy is what they take to be true of the state.[21]

One reason that actual and perceived legitimacy are so often confused may be the influence of modern ideas of the consent of the governed. Yet these ideas, which we ought to remember form simply one family of conceptions of legitimacy among others, are no less dependent on the distinction between the two notions. They regard consent as actually justifying the state's power, not as merely being widely perceived to do so, and they require, for the state to be legitimate, that citizens really do consent to being subject to its rule or really would do so under appropriate conditions.[22] If the state's exercise of power is perceived to be justified or legitimate, then it does enjoy authority: people regard it as having a claim on their allegiance, and its laws are authoritative for their conduct. But neither the rules it imposes nor its power to impose them are then necessarily legitimate. They may not be so, for instance, if the legitimation story the state promulgates and people accept is based on intimidation or on certain sorts of error or illusion. It is true

21. It is often said that Weber made the mistake in question, employing a purely subjective concept of legitimacy and going so far as to suggest that every form of rule (*Herrschaftsform*) that is generally obeyed is legitimate. I believe this interpretation is a mistake. Though he sometimes, for the sake of brevity, referred to enduring forms of rule as being therefore "legitimate," he really meant "regarded as legitimate," for in defining the concept of legitimacy he described every form of rule as involving only a claim (*Anspruch*) to legitimacy. See ibid., I.3.1.
22. For difficulties with the concept of consent, see §7 below.

that from the standpoint of the state's leaders or officials the important thing is often not so much that it really be legitimate, but that it be by and large accepted as so. Yet this fact does not undermine the difference between authority and legitimacy. For only if people accept the state as in fact legitimate, will it possess authority.

More needs to be said substantively, however, about the nature of legitimacy. To this end, I turn to the account that Williams presented. It will prove, despite its deficiencies, very helpful. The basic axiom of his political realism, as I have noted, is that "the first political question" must be the securing of order and the conditions of social cooperation in the face of ubiquitous conflict. It was his reason for regarding legitimacy and not justice as the primary normative notion with which political philosophy should be concerned. In reality, I would note, this only follows if one adds, as Williams did not, that the nature of distributive justice is one of the principal sources of social conflict; otherwise, it could be argued that legitimacy, however much it constitutes the first political question, cannot be defined without reference to an antecedent notion of justice. Such a view is an example of the ethics-centered conception of political philosophy that I argued against in the previous chapter. But let us continue to survey what he had to say about legitimacy itself.

Legitimacy, Williams held, is in addition an indispensable concept since coercion alone—"one lot of people terrorizing another lot of people"—cannot provide a solution to that basic problem of guaranteeing order and social cooperation:

> If the power of one lot of people over another is to represent a solution to the first political question, *something* has to be said to explain (to the less empowered, to concerned

bystanders, to children being educated in this structure, etc.) what the difference is between the solution and the problem, and that cannot simply be an account of successful domination. (IBD, 5; also 63)

This "something" is a legitimation story by which those in power seek to show that their possession of the power they exercise is justified or legitimate. Williams no doubt assumed as well, without mentioning it explicitly, that order and social cooperation can only be secured if this story, or a similar rationale, is widely, if not universally, believed by those in the society who are subject to the regime. For these reasons, then, he devoted considerable attention to how the concept of legitimacy should be understood. This meant—though, as we will see, he was less clear about the distinction than he should have been—that his concern was to explain, not only why the state must seek to be perceived as legitimate, that is, for it to enjoy authority, but also what it is, in at least a general way, for the state to be in fact legitimate.

About the nature of legitimacy he made a number of important points, though I do not think they all are correct. His two most notable theses are the following. Legitimacy, he held, is an essentially historical category. What it is for a system of political rule to be legitimate (not merely to be thought legitimate) has not always been the same. It has not in particular always fit the liberal conceptions current today, but has instead varied from one historical era to another. This rather novel contention is a good example of what I described earlier as the realist desire to see liberalism from the outside, as one political conception among others, like them historically conditioned. It is a thesis with which I agree, though it needs to be clarified and sharpened in certain respects. But his second main thesis, namely the assertion that political legitimacy does not derive from "a morality prior to politics," it will not be surprising that I reject. The claim or belief that some political system is legitimate must rest on an appeal to principles of a moral character, principles specifying with what right and in what regards this system may exercise coercive power and what people it may rightly regard as being subject to its rule. All the same, the considerations that led him to this view, though he mistook their import, are exactly right. This is why I propose to develop further the concept of legitimacy by examining in tandem what Williams had to say on the subject.

4. Legitimacy and Authority

Before taking up his two principal theses, however, we need to examine a core element of Williams's account of legitimacy. This is the idea of the "basic legitimation demand" or BLD, as he dubbed it. Unfortunately, there is considerable ambiguity about just what he meant by the BLD. To clarify the matter, let us begin with the initial point he had in mind. In endeavoring to secure order and the conditions of cooperation, the state, Williams claimed, "has to offer a justification of its power to each subject," a subject of the state being "anyone who is in its power, whom by its own lights it can rightfully coerce under its laws and institutions" and from whom "it expects allegiance" (IBD, 4; also 95 and 135–36). Why is it, one might ask, that the state "has to" offer a justification of its power to each individual satisfying these three conditions? We have in effect already seen the reason. The state cannot fulfill its primary function of ensuring the conditions of social cooperation unless its laws are widely accepted as settling the crucial conflicts in the society, and its laws will not be regarded as thus having authority unless people in the society by and large consider the state to be entitled to the coercive power it exercises to this end. Power by itself cannot generate the necessary authority, or in the adage Williams himself liked to invoke in this regard, "might is not right" (IBD, 5, 23, 135). The state must offer a justification of its power if it is to hope to acquire the authority it needs.[23]

This "must," of course, is a normative "must." States, past and present, that have not sought at all to justify their rule to those subject to their control are only too familiar. These are states whose agents, as Williams said, are essentially engaged in terrorizing the population, in extorting, plundering, and murdering the people at their mercy. Far from providing a solution to the "first political question," such states only compound the problem. Conflict is rife, order is evanescent, and social cooperation is primitive at best. Only if a state seeks to solve the basic problem of social life, must it offer a justification of its exercise of coercive power. Even then, however, social cooperation can be fostered, as history abundantly shows, if the justification offered requires the brutal oppression of part of the population—a slave class, for instance—for the profit of the rest of society.

Now as to what Williams understood to be the "basic legitimation demand," his various remarks oscillate between three distinct possibilities. There is first the demand—just discussed— that the state offer some justification of its rule; second the demand that this justification be by and large accepted by the population, so that the state can enjoy authority; and third the

---

23. As I pointed out in the previous section (and see also chapter 1, §5), people may regard a state as legitimate for reasons different from those the state itself issues. But this is not an eventuality on which the state can rely, and in the rest of this book I shall have little more to say about it.

demand that the justification be in fact correct, so that the state can count as in fact legitimate. Williams never explicitly distinguished between these three different demands. Some of his formulations suggest that the BLD is the first of them:

> Those who claim political authority over a group must have something to say about the basis of that authority.... This requirement on a political authority we may well call the Basic Legitimation Demand. (IBD, 135)

In general, however, he appears to have meant the second— "Meeting the BLD can be equated with there being an 'acceptable' solution to the first political question" (IBD, 4)—or more often the third—"Meeting the BLD is what distinguishes a LEG [legitimate] from an ILLEG [illegitimate] state" (IBD, 4). However, it is also true, as I will explain, that he tended to run together these two latter demands since he failed as well to discriminate clearly between the two concepts of authority and legitimacy.

Williams made a number of points about the BLD that, once the notion has been disambiguated and the difference between those two concepts properly registered, shed considerable light on the nature of political legitimacy. The most fundamental is that the BLD "does not represent a morality prior to politics. It is a claim that is inherent in there being such a thing as politics" (IBD, 5, 7). This is true of the BLD itself in all three possible senses. None of the three demands I distinguished is imposed on political life from the outside, by well-meaning persons for instance who have their own ideas about what politics should be like. Instead, they are each demands the state itself must understand as arising from its primary function of securing order and the bases of social cooperation. For it cannot succeed in this task unless the laws it institutes are viewed as being in its legitimate power to impose, which means that it must offer a justification of its rule, a justification that meets with wide acceptance among the people subject to its rule and that is therefore regarded by them as indeed legitimating the state in its exercise of the coercive power at its disposal. That the very nature of political life gives rise to basic norms of this sort is an important though neglected truth.

Whether the state is in fact justified in its rule is naturally a further question. It is also not evident, as I have observed, that Williams himself quite saw the difference between authority and legitimacy. But most of all it is crucial to note that a demand and the satisfaction of a demand are not the same thing. It is true that the BLD does not in itself represent a morality prior to politics. However, the satisfaction of the BLD (in all three senses) is a different matter. As I have said previously,[24] the legitimation story propounded by the state, people's acceptance of some such story, and the state's legitimacy itself, if it is legitimate, must all rest on what are taken to be or on what in fact are antecedent principles of a moral character, explaining why the state is entitled to exercise coercive power over the community. This fundamental fact Williams also failed to perceive, and I will return to it shortly (§6).

However, two further claims he made with regard to the BLD are on the mark.[25] The first is that the state must address its justification only to those whose allegiance it seeks to command. There may be some inhabitants—Williams mentioned

---

24. See chapter 1, §5, and the beginning of the present chapter.

25. Edward Hall brings out both these points well in "Bernard Williams and the Basic Legitimation Demand: A Defence," *Political Studies* 63 (2015): 466–80, 471, 473.

the Helots of ancient Sparta, but one could add slaves in general or simply resident aliens—over whom a state intends to exercise its power without claiming to possess in their regard a legitimacy they should acknowledge. It seeks their submission, not their allegiance, since it considers them to be subjugated peoples, visiting foreigners, or property rather than persons, not full-fledged members of the society. To be sure, the state claims that the power it exercises over them is legitimate. But it does not intend that its justification for the claim be one that they endorse. It does not seek their approval.

Second, it is not necessary, Williams maintained, that everyone, every "subject," to whom the state does address its legitimation story accept that story or accept enough of it to recognize the state as legitimate (IBD, 135–36). That, he said, would be an unrealistic requirement, since some are bound to be anarchists, bandits, or—most pertinently from a philosophical perspective—people whose ethical or religious convictions are insuperably opposed to the terms in which the state is claiming to justify its power. It cannot be hoped that there exist "absolute or universal conditions of legitimacy, which any 'reasonable' person should accept." For any idea of reasonableness invoked to this end is in reality a historically specific conception that some particular groups happen to share but others do not.[26] What is necessary, he claimed, is that "a substantial number of the people"—including various important groups, young people, influential critics, and so forth, though "it all depends

26. The notion of reasonableness that I myself employ in this book—exercising one's general capacities of reason in good faith and to the best of one's abilities—is indeed universal, but that is precisely why I do not claim that the liberal principle of legitimacy I ultimately propose is one every reasonable person can see reason to endorse.

on the circumstances"—accept the legitimation story provided by the regime (IBD, 136). So long as its authority is thus widely acknowledged, the bases of social cooperation will be assured and a solution to the first political question provided.[27]

Williams did not say much to defend this second point, though he made it clear that he was in particular criticizing the many liberal theorists who have supposed that a liberal regime, if constructed properly, would be one that everyone, given their basic understanding of what is valuable in life, could see reason to endorse. I concur. As I have already pointed out (§1), that notion is an illusion. Every political regime, however inclusive it aspires to be, necessarily excludes. What Rousseau designated as the fundamental problem of politics—to find a form of political rule to which all can freely assent—has no solution.[28] Moreover, liberal ideas of the consent of the governed form one conception of legitimacy among others. It should not be assumed at the outset that this conception, whatever its validity in the modern world, constitutes the standard for every historical epoch.

27. To those who then reject its legitimacy the state will thus stand in a solely coercive relation. Yet this does not mean, contrary to Matt Sleat (*Liberal Realism*, 113, 122–23), that for Williams its exercise of power over them must therefore be illegitimate. Its legitimation story may after all be valid. It is true, as I go on to explain, that no regime can count as legitimate unless it enjoys authority among a substantial number of the members of the society. But that is being assumed in this case. In short, the view that Sleat is here concerned to argue against Williams, namely that a legitimate regime may exercise over some of those from whom it seeks allegiance a rule that consists solely in "successful domination," is a view that Williams accepted. It is, moreover, in my view correct.

28. Jean-Jacques Rousseau, *Du contrat social*, I.6, in *Oeuvres complètes* (Paris: Gallimard, 1964), 3:360. More on this point in the next chapter (§4).

To this last, "historicist" thesis, which is central to Williams's political realism, I return shortly. But first I want to emphasize that the acceptance of a regime's legitimation story by a substantial number of the people concerned serves by itself only to guarantee that regime's authority. It does not suffice to give it legitimacy. "A substantial number of the people" is the answer Williams gave to the question, "Who has to be satisfied that the Basic Legitimate Demand has been met?" That is a very different question from "What has to be true for the Basic Legitimation Demand to be met?" if the BLD is understood as the demand that the state's wielding of coercive power be in fact justified or legitimate. Williams's remarks often elide the difference between those two questions, as when he defined "meeting the BLD" first as "what distinguishes a LEG from an ILLEG state," only then to add, two sentences later, that it "can be equated with there being an 'acceptable' solution to the first political question" (IBD, 4). But authority and legitimacy, between which he thus failed to sharply distinguish, are not at all the same. Perceived legitimacy and legitimacy itself should not be confused since otherwise, as I have observed before, no sense can be made of what it is that people are accepting when they accept that the state is legitimate. What they are accepting is that the state is indeed justified in exercising coercive power over them, and obviously not that they perceive it to be justified—even if its being justified may, when the notion of legitimacy happens to be a liberal one, consist in their consenting or having from their point of view reason to consent to its rule.

It might be thought that Williams would have rejected the distinction between authority and legitimacy (as I have defined them) because of his well-known view that the only reasons a person can be said to have are "internal" reasons. But this is not so. Williams defined internal reasons as those a person could come to acknowledge by a "sound deliberative route" from his existing beliefs and motivations.[29] There is thus a difference, even in the domain of internal reasons, between believing one has a reason to think or do something and actually having such a reason: one's belief may be the product of unsound reasoning. Accordingly, people perceiving a state to be legitimate— that is, its enjoying authority—is not equivalent to their actually having a good or sound reason, given their perspective, to think it legitimate—that is, to its possessing legitimacy.

Nonetheless, authority and legitimacy, though distinct, stand in a particularly close relation to one another, and it is the closeness of this relation that may have sometimes led Williams to miss or neglect the difference between the two concepts. No state can be legitimate unless (among other things) it in fact succeeds in establishing order and the conditions of social cooperation. Yet that is possible only if a substantial number of the people—at least of those having some power or resources— regard the rules the state imposes as rightly binding on their conduct. Legitimacy requires therefore that the state be largely perceived as legitimate. In other words, authority is a necessary condition for legitimacy. It is not, however, a sufficient condition as well. The two concepts remain distinct. For a state is legitimate only if its rule over a group of people is in fact justified and not simply because they think it is justified.

After all, their belief in its legitimacy may be the result of the state's very efforts to legitimate itself. Invoking what he called (in an allusion to the *Ideologiekritik* of the Frankfurt School)

---

29. See Bernard Williams, "Internal Reasons and the Obscurity of Blame," in *Making Sense of Humanity* (Cambridge: Cambridge University Press, 1995), 35. For my own views about internal and external reasons, see *The Autonomy of Morality* (Cambridge: Cambridge University Press, 2008), 58–59, 125–26.

"the critical theory principle," Williams himself held that the state cannot count as legitimate if the people's acceptance of a legitimation story "is produced by the coercive power which is supposedly being justified." He also acknowledged, however, the difficulty in spelling out the relevant sense of "produced by" (IBD, 6). For not only is allegiance always to some extent the result of the state's cultivation, but the reasons the state has through its various institutions inculcated in people for accepting its rule may, in part anyway, be sound ones. Moreover, perceived and actual legitimacy may diverge even when intimidation is not involved. The justification of its rule propounded by the state and accepted in the society can also be defective in virtue of resting on various sorts of errors or illusions, such as notably the failure to realize that better forms of political organization are in the given circumstances available.

All the same, it is important to recognize that legitimacy, though not the same as authority, still depends on it. Since the overall relation between the two concepts is somewhat complex, let me review it again. The state must seek to justify its rule if it is to achieve the authority, the acceptance of its right to institute binding rules in the society, that is necessary if order and social cooperation are to be possible to any significant extent. For that reason, it must address its claim of legitimacy only to those within its territory whom it considers to be full-fledged members of the society, for it is their allegiance alone that it seeks. From others (e.g., resident or visiting aliens) it demands merely submission. For the same reason, it needs to secure acceptance of its legitimacy, not from all those whose allegiance it seeks in principle, but only from enough of them that it acquires the authority it requires. Now no state can actually be legitimate, that is, justified in its rule, unless it succeeds in the task of assuring order and the bases of social cooperation. So legitimacy presupposes authority. Yet authority, the general perception that the state is legitimate and that its laws are therefore binding, is only a necessary and not also a sufficient condition for legitimacy. That is clear simply from the fact that what people hold when they take a state to be legitimate is that it really is legitimate and not that they take it to be so.

5. Legitimacy and History

Having clarified further the relation between legitimacy and authority, I turn to the nature of legitimacy itself. On this score Williams advanced, as I noted, two fundamental theses, each deserving close attention. The first rejects the common assumption that legitimacy is a historically invariant category, that there exists some unchanging standard of what it is for a state to be justified in its rule. Williams was especially concerned to deny that liberal notions of legitimacy apply to every historical epoch, a postulate that cannot help but entail that there has never been a legitimate regime in human history until (at best) quite recently (IBD, 8, 10, 135). There is little point, he quipped, "imagin[ing] oneself as Kant at the court of King Arthur" (IBD, 10). In modern societies—"now and around here," as Williams liked to say—a liberal conception does form the appropriate standard. It "makes sense" under modern conditions. But under different historical conditions, different conceptions of political legitimacy "make sense." By "making sense," Williams seems to have meant "appearing to be justified" to those whose conceptions they are or were, since he maintained that it is not a "normative" concept—our belief that some conception of legitimacy makes sense in a given society does not, he claimed, generally imply that it should guide our own conduct—except when we use it about a state to whose rule we are ourselves subject (IBD, 10–11). For if we say that the legitimation a state gives for its rule over us makes sense to us, we are saying we ought (all else being equal) to acknowledge its claim on our allegiance. Such is the notion of something "making sense" to a person—its appearing to be justified from that person's perspective—that he employed in other writings as well.[30]

Yet this notion of making sense is inadequate to the task at hand. Clearly Williams wanted to say that nonliberal regimes in earlier historical epochs may not have simply appeared legitimate to the people at the time but sometimes were so, and this is indeed a normative proposition: it holds that such regimes were justified in the circumstances, that people were then right to accept them. For otherwise one could still assert the very thing he was keen to reject, namely that only more or less liberal regimes have ever been actually legitimate. It may be true (as I believe it is) that in general a person is justified in believing or doing something if she sees from her perspective a reason there in fact is to believe or do it.[31] Such a view of justification would have been welcome to Williams himself in that he held "internal" reasons to be the only sort of reasons a person can be said to have. I should note that about this last point I do not in fact agree, since a person, it seems to me, can have a reason—a so-called external reason—to believe or do something that she is not in a position to grasp by deliberation from her point of

30. See Bernard Williams, *Truth and Truthfulness* (Princeton, NJ: Princeton University Press, 2002), 233–40, esp. 236, where he writes that someone "may come to think that he acted unreasonably, but he understands why he did so; in such a case he applies to himself much the same interpretive and explanatory schemes as he might apply to someone else. We can say that it makes sense to him now that he acted in that way, though it would not make sense to him to act in that way now."

31. For more on this "contextualist" idea of justification, see §2 of the following chapter.

view.[32] However, reasons of this sort do not bear on whether she is justified in thinking or acting as she does, and since justification is the present concern, let us focus solely on internal reasons. Then we must still distinguish, as I emphasized in the previous section, between there appearing to someone to be such a reason—that is, her thinking she sees such a reason—and there really being one to be seen, one she grasps from her perspective through some kind of sound deliberation. Only in the latter case is she justified in her belief or action. Consequently, a legitimation story "making sense" to people, that is, their perceiving the state to be legitimate and the state thus enjoying authority, is not at all the same thing as the state actually being legitimate. Here then is another case of Williams having failed to distinguish carefully between the concepts of authority and legitimacy.

But let us leave aside misleading formulations and focus on Williams's real intent, which was to claim that the nature of legitimacy depends on the historical situation. I believe this thesis is true. Yet he never properly explained why it is so. He offered a Weber-inspired list of the modern social conditions that make a liberal conception of legitimacy appropriate today— "organizational features (pluralism, etc., and bureaucratic forms of control), individualism, and cognitive aspects of authority (*Entzauberung*)" (IBD, 9). But he did not explain why they call for that conception, or why different conditions might require a different conception.

I think it is possible to do better. First, though, I should make clear the idea at stake, which is that the very standards of legitimacy change with the historical situation. This idea is not to be confused with the obvious fact that whether some regime is legitimate or not depends on historically contingent circumstances. No state, for instance, can be legitimate unless it succeeds in ensuring the bases of social cooperation, and the authority it needs to achieve that end turns on what happen to be the interests and expectations that impel people at the time to accept it as legitimate. This sort of historical variability is an invariant component of the concept of legitimacy. Yet as I explained earlier (§4), perceived legitimacy, though a necessary, is not also a sufficient condition for the state to qualify as legitimate. And it is precisely the further conditions to be satisfied that make the standard itself of legitimacy subject to change as historical circumstances change. This becomes clear when we reflect that the existing level of cultural, economic, and technological development, plus the prevailing assumptions it engenders about what is socially feasible, define the kinds of social cooperation the state can seek to guarantee. These are the materials with which it must work. It is true, of course, that these givens are to an important extent the result of previous state action. However, the work of guaranteeing order is never over: the settlement of past conflicts is likely to occasion new ones, which have to be authoritatively settled in turn and now under altered circumstances. The ways, therefore, in which the state can justifiably exercise its power so as to secure the bases of social cooperation depend on the current range of possibilities of cooperation. To this extent, what counts as legitimate rule cannot but change over history.

Here are two examples to illustrate the way that standards of legitimacy are shaped by the givens of the historical context. First, consider why it must seem silly to brand ancient city-states or empires as illegitimate simply because they rested on the institution of slavery, even though we would doubtless regard as illegitimate any regime that did so in the modern world and may very well believe slavery to be unjust whenever it occurs. The reason is that slavery formed an integral part of every more than rudimentary form of economic organization that had appeared until then, so that nearly everyone in antiquity— given the historical experience at their disposal—reasonably supposed that the conditions of social order and cooperation, at least in any economic system worth having, could not be ensured without incorporating it in some form or other.[33] Certainly chattel slavery was often regarded as unjust, as a misfortune that could befall people or into which they were born without their having deserved it in the slightest. All the same, it was as an institution generally regarded as an economic necessity.

And second, consider the distinctive features of modern society that Williams listed as calling for a liberal conception of legitimacy. Williams did not, as I noted, explain why they do so, nor did he define very clearly that liberal conception itself. But let us adopt the definition I sketched earlier (§1) according to which the state's exercise of power must be based on principles that all members of the society can see reason to endorse, on the assumption (perhaps in some cases counterfactual) that they believe their political life should be organized in such a way. This conception appears eminently suitable for a society characterized by the coexistence of many different cultural traditions ("pluralism"), the substitution of bureaucratic administration for relations of feudal dependence, the pervasiveness of individualist modes of thought, as well as the increasing acceptance of a scientific, *entzaubert* conception of the world and

---

33. On how society for the ancients was unimaginable without slavery, see M. I. Finley, "Was Greek Civilization Based on Slave Labor?," in *Economy and Society in Ancient Greece* (New York: Viking, 1982), 97–115. See also Bernard Williams's own reflections on this subject in *Shame and Necessity* (Berkeley: University of California Press, 1993), 106–29.

with it the transformation of religion from an instrument of social cohesion into a matter of personal faith. For in such a complex, heterogeneous society the conditions of cooperation can be ensured only if the basic rules of social order the state imposes are ones that its members can on reflection, from their now very different perspectives, see reason to accept.

6. The Moral and the Political

In filling out the concept of political legitimacy, I have so far largely endorsed Williams's views, though not without making some significant corrections. Now I come to a major disagreement. It concerns his second principal thesis about the nature of legitimacy. Just like the Basic Legitimation Demand, so legitimacy itself, he argued, does not depend on a morality prior to politics (IBD, 5, 7, 9). This thesis played a key role in defining the sort of political realism he sought to develop. For it led him to hold that political philosophy should, without qualification and in every regard, reject "the priority of the moral over the political" (IBD, 2, 8).

"Political moralism," as Williams rather invidiously labeled the approach he thus opposed, views political life as essentially a realm in which moral conceptions of the ideal society are to be implemented. This project of applying morality to politics has taken in modern times two basic forms, he observed: the aim can be either to bring about certain human goods (this he termed the "enactment model," whose paradigm is utilitarianism) or to create fair structures of social coexistence constraining what states and individuals may do (the "structural model," typified by contractarian theories of justice such as that proposed by Rawls) (IBD, 1–2). Both currents fail, he charged, to appreciate what is distinctive of the political realm. I have already indicated the extent to which I share this criticism, despite the disagreement just signaled. In order to make clear where we part ways, it will therefore be useful if I run through again briefly the main points on which our conceptions of political philosophy largely coincide.

The political realm, so Williams and I agree, is a domain defined by opposing forces and deep disagreements, about—I would emphasize—morality among other things, and its primary concern must therefore be the institution of a common authority. The state can only acquire this authority, however, if it provides a justification of its rule that a substantial number of those whose allegiance it seeks can accept as legitimating its exercise of power. This requirement is the root of what Williams meant by the basic legitimation demand (the BLD), which, as he rightly claimed, "does not represent a morality which is prior to politics." It is instead a demand that is "inherent in there being such a thing as politics" (IBD, 5, 8). Given this understanding of its domain, political philosophy cannot then simply launch into a discussion of the principles of a just society, as is commonly done today. It becomes indeed a kind of applied moral philosophy if it sets out by developing an account of the moral ideals that should be realized in society, moral philosophy having as its object the very nature of the good and the right. Instead, political philosophy must start with what I earlier called the circumstances of politics (§2): the need for social cooperation and the various kinds of conflicts, including not least disagreements about the good and the right, that stand in its way. This is why its primary concern must lie, not with the question of social justice, but instead with the question of authority and legitimacy. The point is not simply that it should concern itself with both. On the contrary, the one question is prior to the other. For the conditions under which the state is justified in exercising its coercive power *constrain* what may count from a political point of view (in contrast to the standpoint of morality as such) as the ideal of social justice to be pursued. The morally best may not be politically justifiable, that is, it may not be legitimate.

Yet what about the concept of legitimacy itself? Does it really stand free from assumptions involving a morality prior to politics? Williams declared that the state's obligation to provide a justification of its exercise of power (one sense of the BLD) does not embody any such assumption since it inheres in the very terms of political existence. That is so. However, he was wrong to suppose that the same holds true of the justification it provides or, if the justification is valid, of the legitimacy the state then enjoys.

Whatever the specific legitimation story may be, whether it invokes some mythical founding, God's purposes, the citizens' consent, or the leader's charisma, it must have an essentially moral basis.[34] For as I have emphasized both in the previous chapter (§5) and in this one (§3), it has to appeal to principles identifying *with what right* the system of political rule wields coercive power over its subjects, in what areas of social life it may *justly* exercise this power, and over what people it *rightly* has jurisdiction. Because, as I have also said, the standard of legitimacy depends on the historical context, these principles do have to fit with the existing level of social and economic development as well as with the conceptions of social life that

34. Note that what embodies a morality prior to politics is in the first instance the legitimation itself the state presents, and not simply our own judgment about whether the legitimation satisfies the BLD. Edward Hall ("Bernard Williams and the Basic Legitimation Demand," 470, 476) confuses these two things in his criticism of the version of this argument I presented in an earlier article "What Is Political Philosophy?," *Journal of Moral Philosophy* 10, no. 3 (2013): 291–92.

are possible at the time. So it would be a mistake to suppose that they hold universally. All the same, they must be presumed to express a morality *prior to politics*. They have to be understood, that is, as possessing a validity antecedent to the authority the state may exercise, since this is precisely what they serve to justify. Because legitimacy consists in a legitimation story being valid, it must therefore have a moral foundation. It cannot, for instance, be understood purely procedurally, as the fact that a state exercises its power in conformity with law.[35] Legitimacy has to do with whether the legal system itself, as a body of rules asserted to be binding on a given group of people and backed up by coercive sanctions, constitutes a justifiable constraint on their conduct.

The moral principles at the basis of a state's proclaimed, perceived, or actual legitimacy need not, it is true, comprise a comprehensive vision of the good and the right. Nor need they imply an overall account of social justice. Such views, which also dominate ethics-centered conceptions of political philosophy, have indeed generally prevailed in past societies and continue to be widespread today, as I discussed in the previous chapter (§§3–4). But as it becomes apparent how easily reasonable people can disagree about substantive ethical questions, legitimation stories may focus instead on what I have called the circumstances of politics and thus concern themselves solely with the conditions under which state power may justifiably be

---

35. Such is the account of the legitimacy of modern states advanced by Niklas Luhmann in *Legitimität durch Verfahren* (Neuwied: Luchterhand, 1969). I agree with Jürgen Habermas's critique of this position in his book *Legitimationsprobleme im Spätkapitalismus* (Frankfurt: Suhrkamp, 1973), though I do not believe he is right to hold (138) that the basis of their legitimacy lies simply in the "Grundnormen vernünftiger Rede" ("the basic norms of rational speech"). For my doubts about his "discourse ethics," see *Autonomy of Morality*, chapter 6, §8.

exercised. Nonetheless, the justification they provide must still
rely on principles of a moral character. A good example is the
liberal conception of legitimacy I outlined earlier (§1), which
holds that the state's use of coercion, its use and threat of force,
is justified insofar as it honors a principle of respect for persons.

I have presented this counterargument in terms of what the
legitimation offered by the state entails and not in terms of
what the state must actually believe. The organs of the state are
often, to varying degrees, disingenuous about the legitimacy
they proclaim, hoping to secure the state's authority one way
or another, by hook or by crook. But what matters here is the
concept of legitimacy itself, however it may be deployed in
reality. On that score, it seems clear that claims to legitimacy
must always rest on assumptions expressing a morality prior
to politics. So clear is it that Williams himself, when he turned
to consider the liberal notion of legitimation modern states invoke, could not help but effectively acknowledge the fact, observing that it may appeal to "an ethically elaborated account
of the person" (IBD, 8) and, more broadly, that discussions
about whether modern state power is legitimate typically refer
to "moral" concepts among others (IBD, 11). Such passages do
not show that Williams's position was more sophisticated than
I have been supposing,[36] but rather that it was inconsistent.
Had he pursued such thoughts a bit further, he would have
seen that liberal legitimation stories invariably invoke moral
principles assumed to have a prior validity and that they are

36. This appears to be Matt Sleat's view in his defense of Williams against this
argument as presented in the article of mine cited in footnote 34. See his "Legitimacy in Realist Thought: Between Moralism and *Realpolitik*," *Political Theory* 42,
no. 3 (2014): 319.

not unique in this regard, but exemplify an inherent feature of the concept of legitimacy.

This critique leaves untouched the reasons Williams rightly had for rejecting in other respects "the priority of the moral over the political." To the extent that much of contemporary political philosophy exemplifies the features in question, it deserves his label of "political moralism." Political philosophy ought not to be understood as a province of moral philosophy, or in Williams's words as a kind of "applied moral philosophy, which is what in our culture it is often taken to be" (IBD, 77). It should not proceed by laying out a body of moral truths about the nature of the good society that are then, so far as possible, to be given political realization. It must instead begin with the problem of legitimacy, with the ubiquity of conflict (over moral questions among other things) and the need for authority if the conditions for social order and cooperation are to be secured. In order to establish itself as the source of such authority, the state has to provide a justification for the coercive power it exercises in pursuing these primary ends, if not further ends as well. This demand for legitimation (the BLD) arises therefore, as Williams said, only within a political situation, in which a state is claiming and expecting allegiance from its subjects. Insofar as the BLD can be said to constitute a moral obligation for the state to fulfill, it does not therefore represent a morality prior to politics. It is part and parcel of politics itself at its most basic level.

It is imperative, however, to distinguish between the demand and the legitimation the state offers to satisfy the demand. The latter, I have argued, does involve a morality prior to politics, inasmuch as it has to appeal to some conception of the conditions under which coercive power may be justly exercised.[37] True, this conception purports to govern how an essentially political problem, the need for authoritative rules to make social cooperation in any significant form possible, is to be handled. But it does so by appealing to principles of a moral character it assumes to possess a validity independent of the political role they are invoked to fill: they serve to legitimate the state's exercise of power in establishing these rules and thus to justify the authority it seeks to enjoy.

7. Degrees of Legitimacy

There remains one further aspect of the concept of legitimacy we need to examine. It is important not only in its own right, but also because of what it helps us to see about the concept as a whole—namely, that legitimacy is always, in the world itself, a matter of degree.

Several times in this (§3) and the previous chapter (§5), I remarked that the legitimacy of a state does not turn solely on its being entitled to exercise coercive power in such ways as enable social cooperation to develop. It must also have the right to impose its rule on the particular people who are subject to its control.[38] Without this further condition, for example, mere

37. In defending Williams against this objection, Sleat ("Legitimacy," 319–22) seems to run together the demand and the state's way of satisfying the demand. I do not deny that the demand for legitimation arises from within the political sphere. Nor, for that matter, did Rawls—with whose "political moralism" Sleat associates me on this score—since his liberal principle of legitimacy (see footnote 10 above) is defined as governing "our exercise of political power."

38. Beginning with his first book, *Moral Principles and Political Obligations* (Princeton, NJ: Princeton University Press, 1979), John Simmons has rightly insisted on the importance of this aspect of legitimacy. In what follows I am indebted to that by now classic work as well as to his later book, *Boundaries of Authority* (Oxford: Oxford University Press, 2016).

conquest could be a legitimate way for a state to expand its domain. If the state had already succeeded in establishing legitimately the necessary forms of social order among a given population, what would count against the legitimacy of its forcing
other people as well into its fold, provided it offered them the
same security and protections of the law? Why would it be illegitimate if present-day Germany, let us say, simply annexed
Alsace, so long as it then treated these new citizens in the same
basic ways it treats its current citizens? One might reply that
this annexation would violate the right of the Alsatians to be
ruled by France. But precisely this right—to which corresponds
the right of France to rule over them—is what we are imagining to be absent. Suppose that Germany were in some sense a
more just society than France or even that France were a less
legitimate state than Germany. That would surely make no difference. Even if such things were true, Germany would still not
be justified in extending its rule over the inhabitants of Alsace
merely because it could do so by force. In this regard too, might
does not make right. People are not legitimately subject to a
state's rule, however successful it may be in establishing the
bases of social order, unless they in particular can rightly be
said to fall within its jurisdiction.

What might a convincing account look like? Under what
circumstances can this condition of political legitimacy count
as satisfied? It is important to remember that not every conception of legitimacy is of a liberal sort and that there can be
historical circumstances in which different conceptions may
be appropriate. Thus, one could imagine Germany taking possession of Alsace, not simply because it can, but on the grounds
that the Alsatians are part of the German Volk, German in language and custom. Such was indeed one of the newly consti-
tuted Reich's justifications for annexing Alsace and Lorraine in

the aftermath of its victory in the Franco-Prussian War. As I have argued, there have been historical circumstances that favored nonliberal conceptions of legitimacy. Perhaps there were then times when legitimate rule could be plausibly founded on its subjects having the same ethnic and linguistic heritage. Clearly, however, any such times were long gone in the Europe of 1871, when, for instance, every country (Germany included) contained people of different extraction and language and many different countries shared the same language. Thus Ernest Renan, in pointing out these facts, argued in a famous essay of 1882 that belonging to the same nation can serve as a basis for legitimate rule only if this belonging is voluntary, only if the individuals involved consent, in a kind of "plébiscite de tous les jours," to being subject to a common authority.[39]

Let us then examine the idea that the state counts as legitimate in the regard in question insofar as the people under its control consent to its rule. The trouble is that, despite Renan's apparent confidence, the notion of consent, in all its various meanings, does not deliver the desired result. It fails to justify the state in ruling over all the people (and only those) who are commonly considered, by its advocates as well, to be legitimately subject to the state's rule. If by consent is meant express consent, people's voluntary profession of allegiance to a state's right to rule over them, then no state will be entitled to exercise its power over many of those typically taken to be rightfully its subjects. For many have never given their express consent, or they have done so unthinkingly or under compulsion, like pupils in American public schools who are required to recite the pledge of allegiance. And if it is claimed that only the majority

39. Ernest Renan, "Qu'est-ce qu'une nation?," in *Qu'est-ce qu'une nation? et autres essais politiques* (Paris: Presses Pocket, 1992), III, 55.

of the citizenry need give its express consent for a state to have the right to rule over them all, then mere conquest (of some small group of people) can once again become legitimate. It is no good turning to the idea of tacit consent, that is, to the idea that people implicitly consent to a state's rule if they continue to reside in the territory over which the state claims jurisdiction. As David Hume memorably retorted, "We may as well assert that a man, by remaining in a vessel, freely consents to the dominion of the master; though he was carried on board while asleep, and must leap into the ocean, and perish, the moment he leaves her."[40] Many have no choice but to live in the country in which they were born and find themselves. They have not, even implicitly, agreed to its dominion.

What then about the idea of hypothetical consent? Will not these problems disappear if we hold that a state is entitled to exercise power over a particular group of people provided that they all, under appropriate conditions, *would* consent to its rule? The trouble is that this solution does not get us very far. Express and tacit consent (to the extent the latter notion makes sense) generally do suffice to bind people to what they have thus agreed to. Hypothetical consent is different. The fact that someone would under specified conditions agree to some claim on his conduct does not necessarily establish that he is in actuality obligated to comply with it. It does so only if the reasons we suppose he would then have to agree to the claim are also reasons the person now has to abide by it. (To say, for example, that a valid principle of justice is one we would have reason to agree to if we gave our own interests no greater weight than we gave to those of others is just to say that we ought not now give

---

40. David Hume, "Of the Original Contact," in *Selected Essays*, ed. Stephen Copley (Oxford: Oxford University Press, 1996), 283.

greater weight to our own interests in determining what it is just to do.) The concept of a hypothetical contract is but a device of exposition.[41] Yet precisely the point at issue concerns the reasons for which a state may be entitled to claim jurisdiction over some particular group of people and they themselves would be obligated to acknowledge this claim. The question has therefore only been deferred.

Earlier (§1), I formulated the liberal conception of political legitimacy in terms that avoid the obscure notion of hypothetical consent. The formulation I gave was that the fundamental principles of political society, since they are coercive in nature, should be such that all who are to count as subject to them *must (now) be able from their perspective to see reason to endorse them*, assuming a commitment—which some may in fact not have—to basing political association on principles that can thus meet with the reasonable agreement of its citizens. By reasons they can now see from their perspective, I mean reasons that they now have and that are accessible or discernible from their present framework of beliefs and interests. (For more on the relation between "having a reason" and "seeing a reason", see the next chapter, §2.) This conception is intended to cover all three components of legitimacy that I have distinguished: (i) the right with which the state may wield coercive power, (ii) the areas of social life in which it may justifiably thus intervene, and (iii) the people over whom it rightly has jurisdiction. The third component is our present concern (the other two components are discussed in the next chapter). Yet this conception, too, it should be noted, does not specify what reasons people may be able to see from their perspective to accept that

41. Cf. Ronald Dworkin, *Taking Rights Seriously* (Cambridge, MA: Harvard University Press, 1978), chapter 6.

they are rightly subject to the rule of some particular state. How might these reasons be filled in, given the liberal conception just mentioned?

Clearly some persons may see reasons of various sorts to believe that one particular state, among all those that operate by principles they can see reason to endorse, has a rightful claim on their allegiance. To the extent that they therefore freely give it their express consent, the problem is solved. But are there reasons that can register with all the members of professedly liberal societies, such as they exist today, for believing that their particular state has such a claim? The three most plausible answers appeal to territory, fair play, or gratitude. Thus, one might suppose that if a state is legitimate in the other two regards mentioned, (i) and (ii), then it is justified in exercising its rule over the people who live in the territory over which it claims jurisdiction, provided no other equally legitimate state similarly claims dominion over that territory. Yet territorial boundaries change over time, they are contested, and most of all they are (modern liberal societies are no exception) largely the product of conquest. Where territory has been seized, what right can a state have to demand allegiance from its inhabitants? What obligation can these inhabitants, or their descendants, have to acknowledge that state's authority, so long as they do not freely consent to its rule?

Now consider the justification based upon the idea of fair play. This idea holds that when people benefit from some scheme of social cooperation, they ought to do their part in contributing to that scheme and thus in helping it to continue. One might therefore suppose that when a particular state has through its exercise of power ensured the bases of social order, those who benefit from the cooperative schemes it thus makes possible ought to do their part, not only in these various schemes, but also to support the system of state power on which the possibility of cooperation depends. For certainly they have benefited as well from the conditions, such as the rule of law, that the state has provided. There are, however, some signal defects in this argument.

One snag is that practices of social cooperation often extend beyond national borders, though a state is obviously not thought to have a right to demand allegiance from those who live under the rule of other states. But the most important difficulty is that the principle of fair play, at least as formulated, is itself dubious. People may receive benefits from some cooperative scheme without ever having wanted to be part of that scheme. They may, in particular, think, and with reason, that the benefits they receive are not their fair share of the total benefits produced by the scheme, that they have been forced by the superior power possessed by other participants to take part in an oppressive or exploitative practice. Why should anyone be obligated to participate in a cooperative practice and thus to acknowledge the legitimacy of a state that makes it possible, unless they can see reason to freely enter that practice and to willingly accept the benefits they may receive from it? Consider the case of slaves who receive food and clothing from their owners in return for the work they do, but who are compelled to do this work because they are someone else's property, along with all this is held to permit. They have no reason other than duress to do their part in the slave economy and therefore no reason at all to think that the state that makes this possible has any legitimate claim on their allegiance.[42]

42. Recall that I am examining how a *liberal* principle of legitimacy might be filled in to explain why a state is entitled to rule over a particular set of people. In different historical contexts, as I argued before (§5), slavery may not be an illegitimate institution.

If, on the other hand, the principle of fair play is reformulated to include only benefits one can see reason to willingly accept, then it will give, in existing liberal societies, the state a right to exercise its rule over only a limited number of the people who happen to be subject to its control. For there will be many—even though they are not slaves—who are forced by circumstances to take part in various cooperative practices which, despite the benefits they may receive (such as wages for a job), they can see reason to refuse to go along with if only they could. With what right can the state demand their allegiance just because it has made these forms of cooperation possible?

Very similar objections apply to the idea that people who take part in the benefits of social cooperation owe, this time directly, a debt of gratitude to the particular state that makes these benefits possible. Inhabitants of other states can also benefit from the civil peace and prosperity the state in question has fostered. They can indeed feel grateful to that state, since otherwise their own well-being would be diminished. Yet obviously they have no reason to think that that state has any legitimate claim on their allegiance. Furthermore, many people in liberal societies existing today rightly think that the benefits of social cooperation they receive are far less than what they are entitled to. They have therefore no reason to believe that the state that makes this exploitation possible deserves their gratitude or has, at least to this extent, the right to rule over them.

What conclusion should we draw from all these remarks? One response is that we need to do better. We need to develop some further, more sophisticated account that will indeed justify a liberal state, of the sort we find today, exercising its rule over the entirety of that particular group of people (and only them) whom it as well as we, in our everyday understanding, regard as belonging within its jurisdiction. I am doubtful, however, that any such account will succeed. So if I am right, what then should we conclude?

A first conclusion is that very few purportedly liberal states, whatever may be their legitimacy in the other two respects, have been or are now fully legitimate in their claim to exercise power over all those who find themselves in fact subject to their control. The only clear basis of legitimacy in this regard is voluntary and express consent, yet such consent is bound to fall short in its extent. We ought not to be surprised by this result. The history of how states, both ancient and modern, came to rule over the people they claim to be theirs has invariably involved the seizure of land and the violent subjugation of persons. America is no exception, since it could not have come into existence or have prospered without the expropriation and genocide of the indigenous population and without the acquisition and exploitation of slaves.[43] What Marx said about the origins of modern capitalism applies as well to the origins and conduct of political regimes throughout human history, including the modern liberal state: it is a history "written in the annals of mankind in letters of blood and fire."[44]

But a second conclusion is equally necessary. From the fact that no state has ever been fully legitimate, it should not be inferred that no state has ever been legitimate at all. Legitimacy

43. Roxanne Dunbar-Ortiz, *An Indigenous People's History of the United States* (Boston: Beacon Press, 2014); Edmund S. Morgan, *American Slavery, American Freedom* (Norton: New York, 1975).

44. Karl Marx, *Capital*, trans. Ben Fowkes (New York: Penguin, 1990), I.viii.26 ("The Secret of Primitive Accumulation"), 875. See also Hume, "Of the Original Contract," 279: "Almost all the governments which exist at present, or of which there remains any record in story, have been founded originally either on usurpation or conquest, or both, without any pretence of a fair consent or voluntary subjection of the people."

is properly a matter of degree. Express consent, for instance, is far more widespread in some states than in others. The point holds, moreover, for all three aspects of the concept of legitimacy that I have distinguished. All too often it is held, though wrongly, that a state must be either legitimate or illegitimate. That legitimacy is a matter of degree is a very important, though neglected truth.

8. The Permanence of Conflict

To conclude, I want to emphasize that although a state claims legitimacy first and foremost in order to carry out its basic function of containing social conflict and ensuring the conditions of cooperation, one should expect that its legitimacy will itself be subject to conflict. Challenges can first of all arise, as I have just indicated, about whether a state is entitled to rule over some particular group of people, especially when these people or their descendants feel that only violent conquest has placed them within the jurisdiction of that state. But in addition, challenges are bound to arise with regard to the two other components of legitimacy. There will always be some, reasonable people among them, exercising sincerely from their perspective the general capacities of human reason, who will deny that the state is justified in its use of coercive power. Certainly, some will regard the further ends the state may choose to pursue— be it wars, economic expansion, or social justice—as an abuse of power. But even as far as securing order and cooperation is concerned, there can be deep disagreement. Conflict never disappears altogether.

Some people, for instance, may fault the state for lacking sufficient power to accomplish its primary task. Others may accuse it of having amassed far too much. Most significantly, there may be people who reject the terms in which the state claims to be justified in its rule. As I have argued, every conception of legitimacy depends on two sorts of premises. First, there are assumptions about the basic cultural, economic, and technological conditions of the time and thus the kinds of social cooperation that need to be secured (§5). And then, second, there are moral principles defining the right with which the state exercises coercive power, the extent to which it may justly do so, and the people over whom it may claim jurisdiction (§6). Both sorts of premises can become the object of controversy. Obviously, some may regard the moral principles the state invokes as incompatible with their own most cherished convictions. But people may also disagree about what are the basic social, economic, and technological conditions of the age or about the kinds of social cooperation they make possible. (What, if anything, does the catastrophe of "really existing socialism" in the former Soviet Union and elsewhere prove about the real possibility of socialism?) They may even believe these conditions are so defective or dangerous that they must be changed if any regime worthy of their allegiance is to appear. (If democracy requires a public that is factually informed, is it even possible in a world permeated by the Internet and social media?) Such beliefs are not necessarily unreasonable. Existing conditions, however deep-rooted they may be, are not unalterable precisely because they are historical in character.

Contemporary resistance to the liberal idea that legitimate political principles are ones people can see reason to endorse often combines both sorts of objections. Those, for instance, who maintain that in the political realm as elsewhere conformity to God's will outweighs respect for human reason typically regard the modern transformation of religion from a society's essential bond into a matter of personal faith as a betrayal of the very meaning of religion that needs to be reversed. Little is to be gained from dismissing such views as perverse. Every conception of legitimacy, however inclusive it aims to be, also excludes and excludes by virtue of embodying moral and factual beliefs that some people from their perspective will see reason to reject. There is no political community in which some will not understandably feel like strangers. Liberalism's aim cannot be a general reconciliation of individual freedom and political rule, for that is impossible. It must be instead to include and exclude for the right reasons. What those reasons are I examine in the next chapter.

3

Political Liberalism and Legitimacy

IN RECENT YEARS, political liberalism, understood as a form of liberal theory importantly different from the classical liberalism of such great thinkers as Locke, Kant, and Mill, has become a vigorous area of philosophical reflection. The amount written on it, both expository and critical, is now immense. Having helped along with John Rawls to introduce this conception,[1] I am naturally pleased that it has proven so fruitful. But I also see cause for concern. For as political liberalism comes to form yet another industrial site in the great business of academic philosophy, its distinctive motivations and goals as well as the way it continues, while deepening, the liberal cause may be easily lost from sight. In the present chapter I try to counter this danger, laying out, as I see them, the problem to which political liberalism aims to provide a solution, the means—in particular, the moral assumptions—by which it

1. Charles Larmore, *Patterns of Moral Complexity* (Cambridge: Cambridge University Press, 1987), chapters 3–5; John Rawls, *Political Liberalism* (New York: Columbia University Press, 1996). I should note that in subsequent writings I have revised in many respects the conception of political liberalism presented in this early work of mine.

seeks to solve this problem, and the ends it can reasonably hope to achieve by the solution it proposes.

The problem at issue has to do with the conditions under which the use of coercive power to institute the authoritative principles of social life may count as justified. In other words, the distinctive character of political liberalism lies precisely in its concept of legitimacy. As the preceding chapters suggest, this is a sign of how deep-going its reformulation of classical liberalism aims to be. In this regard it provides, moreover, a model of the way I have argued political philosophy should be practiced, for it takes its bearings from precisely those historical developments that show why political philosophy should enjoy a relative autonomy from moral philosophy. Whether it can continue to be an adequate response to our historical situation is a question I take up at the end.

1. Origins

A good way to bring out the idea of legitimacy in question is by explaining why liberalism in general, by its nature and not merely by historical accident, is a *latecomer* among political conceptions.[2] In the past, political association, seeking as it must always do to unite by means of binding rules a group of people for the achievement of collective goals, first took the form of communities organized around some single, authoritative, more or less regimented definition of the human good. Only if people are at one in their own ultimate purposes, so it was supposed, will there be the social cohesion necessary to achieve the purposes of the whole. In premodern times, the

2. I have discussed this point before in *The Morals of Modernity* (Cambridge: Cambridge University Press, 1996), 142–44, 211–13.

dominant ideas of the ends of existence were generally religious in character since the world itself was seen as being as much a realm of superhuman powers to be propitiated as an object of prediction and control. At the same time, those in positions of power were only too eager to encourage such ideas for the more-than-human authority they could themselves draw from them. Politics was thus religious, and religion political. To be sure, reigning views of the human good did not go uncontested. But few believed that society was possible except on the basis of some shared and even sacred definition of the meaning of life. As Lactantius memorably summed up the dogma for the Christian Europe of late antiquity and the middle ages, "it is the fear of God alone that secures the mutual society of men, by which life itself is sustained, protected, and governed."[3]

Why this common, political-theological understanding should have begun to crumble in the sixteenth and seventeenth centuries in Europe is a complicated story.[4] Not just the Renaissance and the Reformation, but medieval developments too—the constant tensions between church and state (*sacerdotium* and *imperium*), the succession of reform movements from the tenth century on that sought to recover the true Christian teaching and gave increasing importance to inner faith and conscience—played an important role. Whatever the full explanation, early modern times saw the ever more widespread realization that people reasoning sincerely and carefully about questions of faith and about the nature of the human good in

3. Lactantius (c. AD 240–320), *De ira Dei*, XII: "Timor igitur Dei solus est, qui custodit hominum inter se societatem, per quam vita ipsa sustinetur, munitur, gubernatur."

4. See the recent account in Mark Greengrass, *Christendom Destroyed: Europe 1517–1648* (New York: Viking, 2014).

general are likely to disagree, often because they differ about what it means in these cases to reason well. To the longstanding problems of political rule—how to tame the passions and settle conflicts among interests in order to secure the conditions of social cooperation—was added the need to rethink the basis of political legitimacy itself, given the breadth of reasonable disagreement about the ultimate ends of life. This problem is not one of mere disagreement about religious and ethical questions and about their implications for the organization of society. That too is an age-old difficulty. At issue was instead the widening recognition that reasonable people, in their very exercise of reason, tend to disagree about these matters. For therein lay a fundamental challenge to the cogency of the attempt any political regime must make, if it is to claim legitimacy, to justify to those subject to its rule the system of powers and rules by which it governs. How is political rule to be legitimated once it is recognized that different people typically see reasons to espouse different and conflicting conceptions of what it is to live well?

Early modern times thus saw as well the emergence of various views about how to handle this new problem, views in particular about how to bypass the profound religious and ethical disagreements and find in such factors as self-interest, a regard for the favorable opinion of others, or a sense of what is right and fair the basis of the principles by which people can live together peacefully and fruitfully. The problem and its solution were a preoccupation of such seminal figures as Bodin and Montaigne, Hobbes and Bayle. They constitute as well the dominant concern of the liberal tradition that began paradigmatically with Locke (though the thinkers just mentioned count among its progenitors) and has undergone further key developments in Kant and Mill and to the present day. The central place in this tradition of theories of toleration attests to the formative role played by the effort to reconceive political society in light of reasonable disagreement about the makeup of the human good.

Now the cardinal principles of a liberal society—principles such as freedom of expression and association, equality before the law, rights of political participation—have to be abstract, since they forego appeal to substantive, culturally specific notions of the human good. Yet if there is to be the mutual trust for people not merely to regard such principles as correct but to accept the special vulnerability that comes with living under a regime where dependence on the compliance of others and subjection to state enforcement no longer rest on a presumed agreement about the ultimate ends of life, they must still understand themselves as indeed *a people*, distinct from other peoples and bound together by a sense of community independent of their acknowledgment of those principles.[5] This common life must be without a common view of what it is to live life well. But it can still revolve around such circumstantial factors as geography and language. And it will certainly and most importantly involve a shared historical experience, centered on the memory of past conflicts, often bloody, which has brought them to the hard-won realization that the substantive ideals that once defined their political existence should now, as abiding objects of reasonable disagreement, cease to have that function. This realization embodies the conviction—its precise moral character will occupy us later on (§3)—that they need to organize their political existence on a basis that precludes appeal to

5. Liberal thinkers have frequently overlooked this need for a prior sense of community. Present-day communitarian thinkers recognize its importance, but wrongly suppose it can only consist in some shared conception of the human good. I shall return toward the end to this political notion of "a people."

such notions. It is a conviction forged by their memory of what the alternative has been.

The various elements of their common life—a shared historical experience and the lessons learned from it, mutual trust, even the fact that they speak the same language—are naturally the results of earlier forms of political rule. Without the existence of authoritative rules instituted by state power, there would be, as I argued in the preceding chapter (§2), little social cooperation. Thus the mutual trust on which a liberal order relies is in large part an inheritance of preliberal times, preserved in ongoing habits of give and take.[6] Yet an equally essential feature of their common life is the memory of past suffering and oppression, when the rules of social life were founded upon some official, generally religious understanding of the human good. If they agree to live under the abstract principles of a liberal order, they must feel united as a people not only by what they have kept, but also by what they have seen good reason to leave behind.

This is why I said at the beginning that liberalism has inherently the character of a latecomer. It belongs to the self-understanding of a liberal political order that it has arrived late on the scene. It would be wrong, of course, to confuse aspiration and reality, to suppose that liberal ideals have become fully achieved in today's "liberal democracies" or to regard "liberalism" as simply a historical category designating the practices Western societies have in fact devised for dealing with reasonable disagreement about the human good. The confusion

6. This is the truth in Ernst-Wolfgang Böckenförde's famous statement that "Der freiheitliche, säkularisierte Staat lebt von Voraussetzungen, die er selbst nicht garantieren kann" (The liberal, secular state is sustained by presuppositions that it cannot itself guarantee) (*Recht, Staat, Freiheit* [Frankfurt: Suhrkamp, 1991], 112).

is frequent among both liberalism's apologists and critics. All the same, liberalism is a political conception that emerged as a response to one of the defining experiences of modern times and that has shaped to a considerable extent the world of today. Even if, as is not true, there were a liberal society without a preliberal past (America was built on the memory of the illiberal institutions and practices of the Old World that had supposedly been left behind), it would still define itself by the need to avoid the lure of trying to organize its political life around some specific religious or ethical vision. Precisely because liberal principles rule out such ways of setting the terms of political association, they allude to the temptation of doing so. Liberalism always presents itself as a better account of the nature of just rule than those we are or have been initially inclined to adopt.

This does not mean that all the different forms of the propensity to align political society on controversial ideals of the human good have been clear from the start. On the contrary, liberal thinkers themselves from John Locke's time to our own have often presented their political philosophy in terms of one or another version of an overarching individualist ethic, committed to cultivating a critical attitude toward inherited forms of belief and cultural traditions, to thinking for oneself and working out on one's own the life one will lead, that is in fact far more disputable than they have supposed.

That liberal thought has taken this path is not surprising. Individualism of this sort has formed a powerful current in our world. It grows out of basic features of modern society, especially the market institutions of a capitalist economy. It is also an understandable response to the expanding recognition, ever since the sixteenth and seventeenth century wars of religion, that reasonable people—by which I mean (here and throughout) people exercising their general capacities of reason in good faith and to the best of their abilities—tend naturally to disagree about the essence of the human good. Classical liberals such as Locke, Kant, and Mill found it therefore plausible to conclude in their different ways that the principles of political society should be based on such an individualist ethic, that these principles should abstract from controversial ideals of the good in order to express thereby the spirit that should shape the whole of our lives. Our allegiance, they believed, to any substantial view of the good—to any concrete way of life involving a specific structure of purposes, significances, and activities, such as a life shaped by certain cultural traditions or devoted to a particular religion—can be truly valuable only if we understand such forms of life as ones we choose, or would choose, from a position of critical detachment. This general individualist perspective formed then the framework in which they developed their political philosophy. (The idea of "individuality" plays this role explicitly in Mill's essay *On Liberty*.) Our status, our rights and freedoms, as political subjects or citizens should be independent of whatever specific conceptions of the human good we happen to espouse because in that way political principles reflect—as Locke, Kant, and Mill might have said respectively—the fallibilist, autonomous, or experimental attitude that we as persons ought to maintain at the deepest level of our self-understanding.

The situation has turned out to be more complex, however. Individualist ideas have themselves become an object of reasonable disagreement. From parts of the Romantic movement to present-day communitarianism, there has developed an appreciation of the significance of tradition to which the premium that individualism places upon critical reflection appears to embody a kind of moral blindness.[7] Is not a distanced and questioning attitude toward inherited ways in reality only one value among others? If so, to give it supreme authority may therefore block recognition of much else that is also of value. Thus it has been held that we can share in the good that some ways of life offer, only if we do not think of our allegiance to them as elective, as a matter of decision, but regard it instead as constitutive of our very sense of what is valuable, as rooted in a feeling of belonging. The importance of common customs, ties of place and language, and religious faith can lie in shaping the very understanding of good and ill through which we make the choices we do. On grounds such as these, liberalism itself, given its attachment to individualist ideals, has often been accused ever since the Romantic era of leading to the dissolution of so-cial bonds and to the impoverishment of moral thinking.[8]

Today, despite the massive influence that individualist modes of thought continue to wield, they are recognized to be notori-ously contentious. No doubt they have always been contested, but now their difficulties and drawbacks are widely acknowl-edged. However we settle to our own satisfaction the respec-tive merits of thinking things out for ourselves and following tradition, we cannot deny that on this question reasonable peo-ple are bound to disagree. Whether these two outlooks are in fact so sharply opposed—whether self-reliance is not nurtured by certain kinds of community and whether any traditional form of life can long endure without innovation—is but a fur-

7. For my more detailed accounts of this Romantic theme, see *The Romantic Legacy* (New York: Columbia University Press, 1996), chapter 2; as well as *Morals of Modernity*, 127–34.

8. A recent example is Patrick J. Deneen, *Why Liberalism Failed* (New Haven, CT: Yale University Press, 2018).

ther dimension of the controversy. Classical liberalism aimed at a sort of neutrality—a neutrality of justification, if not a neutrality of effect—by which the principles of political society would rest on a basis free from disputable conceptions of the human good. "Political authority needs only to be just," Benjamin Constant declared, "we will take care of our happiness."[9] Yet the basis adopted was in fact no less controversial itself. Here, then, liberalism faces a challenge. Should it stand by its classical commitment to some version of an individualist view of life, becoming now an avowedly "perfectionist" doctrine that grounds its political principles upon a comprehensive ideal of human flourishing?[10] Or should it instead, seeing in this new area of controversy yet another instance of that tendency to reasonable disagreement to which it has from the beginning been a response, seek a reformulation that can somehow accommodate the different sides of the dispute? The second path is the one pursued by the political liberalism that John Rawls, I, and others have espoused. It aims to fix the principles of political association in terms independent not only of religious convictions and substantive notions of the good life, but also of ethical ideals defining the sort of attitude—individualist and self-critical or communitarian and traditionalist—that we ought to have toward the ideas of the good we espouse, since they too are ineluctably objects of dispute. These principles

9. Benjamin Constant, *De la liberté des Anciens comparée à celle des Modernes* (1819): "Que [l'autorité] se borne à être juste; nous nous chargerons d'être heureux," reprinted in Constant, *De la liberté des modernes* (Paris: Pluriel, 1980), 513.

10. "Perfectionist" liberalism has indeed become (often under this name) an important strand of contemporary thought. Particularly in its opposition to political liberalism, it took its start in writings of Joseph Raz, for instance in his book *The Morality of Freedom* (Oxford: Oxford University Press, 1986). My reasons for rejecting it are implicit in the positive exposition of political liberalism that follows.

will help to specify, of course, the basic distribution of rights and powers in society. However, first and foremost they will include—for political liberalism as I conceive it fits the more autonomous conception of political philosophy I outlined in the preceding chapters—a definition of the very conditions under which any such framework of social justice may be made legally binding, in other words, a definition of political legitimacy. Given that the proper aim of government from the liberal point of view is not to promote some particular vision of what it is to live our lives well, but instead to establish fair rules and institutions under which people can pursue their various ends (this is the sense of "liberty" or individual freedom at the center of liberalism), the legitimacy of these rules and institutions, whatever they specifically may be, needs therefore to be justified at a more reflective level of neutrality.

Seen in this light, political liberalism does not represent a radical departure from the motivations of its classical forebears. It too seeks to define a form of political society that acknowledges the breadth of reasonable disagreement. The differences stem partly from experience, as it has become clearer just how widely reasonable people can disagree about ethical matters. If, moreover, the core commitments of liberal thought can be shown to be detachable from its classical reliance on an individualist philosophy of life, we can more easily recognize what should have been evident all along. The real motor behind those features of modern individualism that many have deplored has been not so much liberalism as capitalism, whose relentless commodification of the world and turning of social relations into market relations melts all that is solid into air.

Nonetheless, as evinced by its effort to reconceive the liberal conception of legitimate rule, political liberalism would be wrongly understood if one supposed its paramount objective were simply to secure a basis for political association about which all reasonable people can agree. Reasonable disagreement may give rise to the crucial problem to which it offers a political solution. But the solution itself rests upon moral assumptions that, requiring that the nature of political legitimacy and thus the basic terms of social justice be defined without reference to individualist ideas, play this role because they are held to be right and not because they are thought to be universally shared. On this essential point political liberalism is frequently misunderstood (even by some of its proponents), and one of my principal aims is to dispel the confusion.

Before going further in this direction, however, I want to look more closely at the idea itself of reasonable disagreement. Though it has provided, as I have said, the main impetus in the development of liberal thought past and present, it can itself— on reflection—seem a questionable notion.

2. The Key Problem

What, then, is to be understood by reasonable disagreement? It does not mean, as I emphasized before, the simple fact that people disagree and disagree in particular about the nature of the human good. That is a banality, familiar from time immemorial. It is rather the idea that reasonable people, precisely in virtue of exercising their reason in good faith and to the best of their abilities, tend to come to contrary opinions when they consider, especially in some detail, what it is for instance to live well.

The phenomenon itself seems evident enough. How often, for instance, do we believe we agree with others about some important matter of life only to discover, as we discuss the subject further, listen more carefully, and reflect on what has been said, that we are in reality quite far from being of the same mind! Perhaps we are all at one in holding that freedom and justice are paramount values. But when we begin to reflect and spell out what we mean by them, we generally find that we are very much at odds, not just with one another but sometimes even with ourselves.

Since, however, it has long been part of our cultural and philosophical tradition to believe that reason ensures convergence of opinion, reasonable disagreement can appear to be a notion hard to make sense of. If people disagree about some subject, given the same evidence, then—so one can feel impelled to think—they cannot all be reasoning correctly. How, therefore, can their disagreement count as reasonable? Once they learn of their disagreement, must they not each, if convinced they are fully reasonable themselves, reckon that the others are not as reasonable as they? Or if they believe they are all equally reasonable, must they not each conclude that the reasons they supposed they had for their views are inadequate and that the proper position to adopt, pending new evidence or further reflection, is to suspend judgment about the matter at hand? Reasonable disagreement can thus look like merely a temporary condition: when people who believe they are equally reasonable discover that they disagree, they would seem obliged to backtrack from their opposing views, and as a result their disagreement would cease.[11]

11. If belief is understood, no longer qualitatively (as an all-or-nothing matter), but quantitatively—in terms of degrees of belief—then reasonable disagreement about some subject among people who recognize one another as equally reasonable and as equipped with the same evidence need not, on this traditional view, lead to suspension of judgment. It may lead only to a lessening of each party's degree of belief or confidence, but to a point still above their threshold for full belief. Yet given that still other equally reasonable people, when the subject is the nature of the

A first reply to this objection is that suspending judgment may not be an option when we are considering, not what to believe about some question of detail, but which path of life to choose or embrace. Then time and circumstance press us to decide one way or the other. We are, moreover, already embarked on the path that is ours at the moment, and the choice whether to continue as we have been or to set out in some new direction is one that, at least implicitly, we cannot escape making.

But in addition and more fundamentally, reasonable disagreement can be seen as likely and as likely to endure when the subject of discussion, in whatever domain, is of sufficient complexity and difficulty. When the key concepts involved can be variously interpreted in plausible but conflicting ways and when the crucial sorts of considerations that bear on the subject can be differently weighted, again in plausible but conflicting ways, people can well come to contrary conclusions if their starting points, that is, the background of existing beliefs, standards, and interests that appear to them pertinent and that shape how they interpret and weigh the evidence, are significantly different. Even when they share the same principles, they thus can differ in their views about what these principles entail in given situations, depending on what else they happen to believe. Their disagreement in all these cases will be reasonable insofar as they have reasoned properly from their respective points of departure. Reasonable views are justified views—that is, views

---

human good, are also likely to disagree with them for different reasons, their degree of belief would have to decrease even further and ultimately to a point below the threshold. So here too, suspension of judgment, on the traditional view, appears inevitable. In the following, I will ignore, for simplicity's sake, the complications involved in the idea of degrees of belief.

one sees reason to accept, given one's other convictions—but justified views need not be true. That is why reasonable disagreement is both reasonable, the different sides each holding justified positions, and a matter of disagreement, the different sides presuming that there is a correct answer to the question that divides them. Here, by the way, I should point out that "seeing a reason," as I use the phrase, entails that there really is such a reason, though a reason one can discern given the terms of one's own perspective, and is thus to be distinguished from the broader category of "having a reason," which covers cases as well in which the reason in question is not a reason one is in a position to grasp.[12]

To return to the objection I first mentioned: Some may think—as does much of the current epistemological work on reasonable disagreement[13]—that when people who consider one another to be equally reasonable realize that they disagree on some matter, despite having before them the same body of evidence, they then ought to change their initial position: they should suspend judgment or revise their conclusions. For they must suppose that someone is making a mistake, and if they re-

12. "Seeing a reason" therefore involves reasons of the sort that have been called "internal" (see chapter 2, §4). Reasons in general, as I conceive them, consist in the way that certain physical or psychological facts count in favor of possibilities of thought and action a person has (see chapter 1, §7). The reasons a person has depend therefore on the possibilities she has, but sometimes a person, given the basic framework of her thinking, is not in a position to see or grasp a reason she has. For detailed expositions of this conception, see *The Autonomy of Morality* (Cambridge: Cambridge University Press, 2008), chapter 3, §3, and chapter 5, §7, as well as two recent German books of mine: *Vernunft und Subjektivität* (Frankfurt: Suhrkamp, 2012); and *Das Selbst in seinem Verhältnis zu sich und zu anderen* (Frankfurt: Klostermann, 2017).

13. See, for instance, David Christensen, "Epistemology of Disagreement: The Good News," *Philosophical Review* 116, no. 2 (2007): 187–217.

gard one another as equally reasonable and as having the same evidence—as "epistemic peers," to use the language of that work—they each have no grounds for ascribing the mistake to the others rather than to themselves. Reasonable disagreement, again it may be thought, ought to induce self-skepticism, so that the disagreement itself will disappear. Yet if, as I have been arguing, being reasonable consists in believing and doing what is justified given one's background beliefs, standards, and interests, then another person's coming reasonably to a different conclusion than we do does not by itself give us a reason to think that our view may be false. A good reason for us to doubt our view must be one we can recognize to be such from our own perspective, and the fact that another person has come to an opposing view by reasoning well, but from different starting points than ours, is not in general that sort of reason.[14] That is why we can also regard the other person's view as reasonable or justified though at the same time wrong, because of the mistakes we see in his underlying premises. (Similarly, historians often characterize past beliefs and actions as at the time reasonable or justified despite being actually false.)

The recent epistemological writings to which I referred can make little sense of the idea of reasonable disagreement because they slight the way the most significant examples turn on reasonable people having different background convictions about how to determine what to believe and do.[15] If they

14. Note that I am talking here about reasons for us to doubt our view and not about reasons why our view may be wrong. This distinction is related to the one between seeing and having a reason that I drew in the previous paragraph.

15. A notable exception to this widespread approach is the essay by Alvin Goldman, "Epistemic Relativism and Reasonable Disagreement," in *Disagreement*, ed. Richard Feldman and Ted A. Warfield (Oxford: Oxford University Press, 2010), 187–215. In it he develops a position that is similar, if not identical, to the one I present here.

happen to mention such factors, they often stipulate that people who differ in this regard cannot regard one another as epistemic peers equipped with the same evidence; as a result, they
define the phenomenon out of existence. Generally, however,
they focus on disagreement in perceptual and mathematical
judgments, in which (in contrast to judgments about the human
good, for instance) background convictions play little role.

To this defense of the idea of reasonable disagreement one
may rejoin that, in the situations described, we cannot regard
other people's views as justified unless we consider their premises to be justified as well and that we therefore cannot coher-
ently think of their views as justified though wrong. Yet this
rejoinder assumes that no proposition can count as justified
unless the beliefs on which it rests are justified as well, and that
assumption, though widespread, seems to me mistaken. Justification, properly understood, is not an activity in which we
engage for its own sake, but rather a response to some problem, to some question or doubt that has interrupted the course
of our routines. While it is certainly a problem whether to
adopt a belief we do not yet hold or whether to modify or reject an existing belief whose truth we have discovered reasons
to doubt—which is why in these cases justification is in order—
the mere fact that we possess some belief is not in itself a problem. We need a reason to open our mind just as we need one to
make our mind up. Beliefs serve to guide our conduct, including the solving of problems, and the proper object of justification is thus not belief itself, but changes in belief. Questions
of justification arise within a context of given beliefs that do
not in and of themselves need to be justified. Such then are the

I also find sympathetic the account in Samantha Besson's wide-ranging book, *The
Morality of Conflict and Reasonable Disagreement* (Oxford: Hart, 2005).

terms in which we should judge, not only our own thinking, but the thinking of others as well. This "contextualist" understanding of justification, as I have called it,[16] makes the phenomenon of reasonable disagreement intelligible, and though it is controversial, I repeat the point I made before (and to which I will return at length): the aim of political liberalism, as I understand it anyway, is not to rise above all controversy.[17]

The factors I have cited to explain reasonable disagreement—that central concepts can be variously interpreted, pertinent considerations ascribed different weight, especially because the way people reason can be differently guided by past experience—correspond to the gist of what John Rawls called "the burdens of judgment" in his own effort to account for reasonable disagreement about moral and political matters.[18] Rawls acknowledged, however, that the burdens he described are not peculiar to the practical domain. Indeed, we may well wonder whether the exercise of reason does not in general breed disagreement about difficult questions. In premodern times, for instance, no two physicists were likely to think the same who thought at all. If the modern sciences tend to achieve a convergence of opinion about complicated matters, might this not be because they have made nature the object of a form of inquiry, based on controlled experiment and measurement, that is geared to making them a cumulative enterprise?

16. For more detail, see *Autonomy of Morality*, 4–5, 12.

17. In his critique of political liberalism's epistemological commitments, David Enoch supposes that it is. See his essay "Political Philosophy and Epistemology: The Case of Public Reason," *Oxford Studies in Political Philosophy* 3 (Oxford: Oxford University Press, 2017), 133–65. Moreover, nowhere in his essay does he consider an account anything like my own of how people can see other people's views as justified from their perspective, yet as wrong by their own lights.

18. Rawls, *Political Liberalism*, 56–57.

What should in any case be clear is that the expectation of reasonable disagreement in regard to moral questions is not itself a moral doctrine but instead a conception of reason's capacities for dealing with these questions. Sometimes people (including Rawls himself) refer to it as "pluralism" or the "fact of pluralism," though confusingly so, if an allusion is intended to the celebrated writings of Isaiah Berlin.[19] The pluralism Berlin advocated is a positive theory about the character of the human good, holding that it does not derive from one single source of value (such as pleasure, freedom, or knowledge), but consists instead in a plurality of ultimate ends, irreducible to any common measure, resistant to any definitive ranking, and liable to come into conflict with one another. Far from being the same thing as the expectation of reasonable disagreement, this theory is, not surprisingly, one more object of such disagreement, a doctrine about whose merits people are bound to differ.

Perhaps value pluralism, if it is true (as I happen myself to believe), may help to explain, at least in many cases, why reasonable people find themselves easily at odds about what it is to live well: they each, we might surmise, see reason for their views because they are responding ultimately to different and incompatible elements of the good. The explanation of reasonable disagreement in the moral domain would thus involve, not only some general features of reason, encapsulated in the so-called burdens of judgment, but also the very nature of the good. That such disagreement should have become, however, so salient and pervasive a feature of the modern world must depend not on universal, but on historical factors. Chief among

---

19. On the differences between the two, see *Morals of Modernity*, chapter 7; and *Autonomy of Morality*, 141–42.

them are surely the great variety of cultural traditions we have inherited, the increasingly complex forms of division of labor in which we live, and the modern practices of toleration themselves, which, in welcoming the expression of differences, have encouraged them to proliferate further. Finally, there are two all-important clarifications about the meaning of the word "reasonable" itself. First, I assume no distinction between "reason" and "faith."[20] That should be evident from what I said earlier about how liberal thought took its start chiefly from an appreciation of how readily matters of religion lend themselves to reasonable disagreement. People of faith, too, typically seek to understand better their convictions, to interpret their faith in the light of their experience, and to integrate it with their other commitments. They pursue questions and deal with doubts, and so they "reason" in the broad sense I intend, even if their distinctive starting points may be allegiance to tradition or belief in revelation.

Second, as my preceding remarks should also have indicated, I mean by reasonable people those who are exercising their general capacities of reason sincerely and to the best of their abilities in determining what to believe and do.[21] Reasonableness, as I use the term here and in other writings in political philosophy, is thus an essentially epistemic notion. This is not,

20. In her critical discussion of my views, Martha Nussbaum ("Perfectionist Liberalism and Political Liberalism," *Philosophy & Political Affairs* 39, no. 1 [2011]: 3–45) complains that I slight religious citizens by presenting political liberalism as engaged centrally with disagreement among reasonable people (32). She therefore quite misunderstands me on this score, presupposing—as in this context I do not—an opposition between reason and faith. See also footnote 45 below.

21. See chapter 1, §4. There is a lot more to be said about the nature of reason and of reasons than is relevant from a political point of view. For my broader and indeed metaphysical views on this subject, see the writings cited in footnote 12.

to be sure, the only way the term may be used, or the only way it has been used in talking about liberalism and its connection to reasonable disagreement. Rawls, for instance, followed a different usage. When turning in his later work to the question of legitimacy, he defined reasonable people as those who both (i) recognize the burdens of judgment and their consequences for political association—namely, that only the oppressive use of state power can unify a society around a single conception of the human good—and also (ii) are disposed to propose and abide by fair principles of cooperation, given that others are similarly disposed.[22] His notion thus combines an epistemic and a moral component, though I should note that the epistemic component—(i)—does not coincide with reasonableness as I define it, but instead designates the awareness of certain consequences of people being reasonable in my sense.

Now, it cannot be denied that in everyday life we often use the term in the moral sense of showing a concern for fairness, particularly in Rawls's sense of that notion, which is that of being willing to cooperate with others on terms based on principles all can see reason to accept.[23] A person is "reasonable," we then say, if she not only can see some disputed matter from the other parties' point of view, but is committed to seeking some common ground for resolving the conflict. In such cases, we may even contrast the reasonable person with someone who is merely "rational," focused on pursuing his own interests efficiently and regarding the viewpoints of others as merely fur-

---

22. Rawls, *Political Liberalism*, 48–62.

23. For Rawls's conception of fairness, see for instance "Justice as Fairness" (1958), in *Collected Papers* (Cambridge, MA: Harvard University Press, 1999), 59; and *Justice as Fairness: A Restatement* (Cambridge, MA: Harvard University Press, 2001), 6.

ther givens of the situation to incorporate into his calculations. This sort of contrast was highlighted by W. M. Sibley in an insightful essay that Rawls invoked as he went on to associate our two distinct moral powers, having a sense of justice and pursuing a conception of our good, with the reasonable and the rational respectively.[24] Because of this difference in what the two of us mean by the term, "reasonable" as I use it has to do with the central *problem* to which liberalism has sought a political solution—the fact that people reasoning in good faith and to the best of their abilities disagree about the nature of the good—whereas Rawls used the term to refer to part of the *solution* itself. I have several reasons for not following Rawls's usage.

If, as I have argued, we cannot fully understand the sources of such disagreement in the moral realm without seeing that it is to be expected in any domain whenever difficult concepts must be interpreted and competing considerations weighed together, then we need a suitably general notion of "reasonable" to characterize reasonable disagreement properly. This notion cannot be specifically moral in character, but must instead be essentially epistemic.

Furthermore, to let a moralized usage of a not obviously moral term such as "reasonable" play a key role in one's political theory—as Rawls did, for he used it to define many of his key concepts such as reasonable comprehensive doctrines, reasonable citizens, reasonable pluralism, and even reasonable disagreement—risks failing to go further and bring out all the moral principles on which the whole theory rests. This is what

24. W. M. Sibley, "The Rational versus the Reasonable," *Philosophical Review* 62, no. 4 (1953): 554–60. Rawls refers to Sibley's essay in *Political Liberalism*, 49.

happened in Rawls's case: he never spelled out clearly the moral basis of his political liberalism.[25] In particular, he never fully explained why—in virtue of what underlying moral principles—reasonableness in the moral sense and fairness as he understood it should serve to ground a conception of political legitimacy.

I think it always best to make as explicit as possible the moral foundations of one's political theory. In this case, the assumptions involved are in fact none other than the basis on which political liberalism seeks to modify the individualist framework of its classical antecedents and reformulate accordingly the liberal conception of political legitimacy. Having explained the nature of the reasonable disagreement to which the liberal tradition has all along been a response, I return therefore to the question of the precise terms in which this response should be developed.

3. Foundations

The impetus for the development of political liberalism has been, I observed, the growing recognition that the individualist ideals on which classical liberalism relied in defining the basis of legitimate rule amidst reasonable disagreement about important religious and ethical matters are understandably an object of controversy in their own right. However, it is important to see that political liberalism is relying on more than simply historical experience in freeing itself from dependence on a view of life that prizes critical reflection, autonomy, and experimentation. It is also drawing upon moral assumptions that imply that this is the proper route to take. Every conception of

25. I examine in some detail his ambiguities on this score in *Autonomy of Morality*, chapter 6.

political legitimacy, as I argued in the preceding chapter, draws upon some moral basis. After all, why should not liberal thinkers instead dig in their heels and, observing correctly that no political conception can accommodate every persuasion (a point to which I shall return), maintain that liberalism stands or falls with a general commitment to individualism? The answer must be that the core motivations of liberal thought lie at a more fundamental moral level. So political liberalism needs to make plain what these underlying convictions are.

How far did Rawls take us in this regard? Political liberalism, he remarked when taking up the question of legitimacy in his later writings, "applies the principle of toleration to philosophy itself." Its goal is a political order whose conception of social justice is "as far as possible, independent of the opposing and conflicting philosophical and religious doctrines that citizens affirm," including those in terms of which liberal principles themselves have often been propounded.[26] For only if citizens can see reason to accept the very basis of a political order are they rightly subject to it and thus to the enforcement of the conception of justice by which it operates. This requirement Rawls went on to formulate as what he called *the liberal principle of legitimacy*: "Our exercise of political power is proper and hence justifiable only when it is exercised in accordance with a constitution the essentials of which all citizens may be reasonably expected to endorse in the light of principles and ideals acceptable to them as reasonable and rational."[27]

---

26. Rawls, *Political Liberalism*, 9–10.

27. Ibid., 217; also 137. In this regard, I remind the reader of my claim that legitimacy is a more basic political concept than justice since it has to do with the exercise of coercive power: a regime is legitimate only if, be the laws it establishes ever so just, its claim to be entitled to impose them by force, if need be, is justified. It is the liberal idea of legitimacy that political liberalism undertakes at bottom to recast.

Let us look more closely at this principle of liberal legitimacy, which I think is on the right track. It can seem akin to
the sort of consent principles not unfamiliar in the liberal tradition. Yet we should note that in referring to constitutional
essentials "citizens may be reasonably expected to endorse," it
makes the legitimacy of a system of political rule depend not
simply on the actual but on what would be the reasoned agreement of the governed. Moreover, the idea in general that certain
norms are valid because they would be the object of rational
agreement really means that there are in fact reasons the parties can all see to accept them (see chapter 2, §7). So the more
direct way to state the principle in question—though I shall
sometimes use the notion of agreement for convenience—is
to say it holds that political arrangements are legitimate provided there are reasons that people can (not necessarily do) all
see from their perspective to endorse them. For my own part, I
would add, importantly, that these need not be the same reasons. One should expect, and regard it as a source of strength,
that there can be different routes to the same core liberal commitments. (This is what we may term a "convergence" rather
than "consensus" view of the reasons making for legitimacy.)

It should also be noted that the principle as stated by Rawls
assumes that the people are, in his sense of the terms, reasonable and rational. On this score—the commitments citizens
must be presumed to have for the reasons they can see to have
a bearing on legitimacy—I will have more to say in the next
section. But leaving this point aside for now, I think that in
other respects Rawls's legitimacy principle does give expression to the abiding heart of the liberal vision, the core conviction in virtue of which its longstanding reliance on individualist forms of thought needs to be abandoned. Let there be no

confusion, by the way, about what this principle is meant to achieve. It is not an axiom from which basic rights and constitutional provisions can be deduced. It serves rather as a constraint they must satisfy. One can therefore expect, as has in fact happened, that different liberal societies will develop in the light of their traditions and experience somewhat different conceptions of what these rights and powers are.

Nonetheless, Rawls's formulation of the liberal legitimacy principle does not go deep enough. Its basis remains unclear. True, this principle endorses itself: it too is a principle that citizens, as it should be understood to characterize them, can see reason to accept. But self-certification is not a justification.[28] The crucial question is, what are the reasons that favor founding political legitimacy on fairness (as he understood it) in preference to other conceptions of legitimacy that, historically, have appealed instead to the will of God, the ways of the forefathers, the cultivation of human excellence, or indeed the development of individuality? All Rawls really tells us, by way of justification, is the following. Reasonable people, on his definition, are said to combine a commitment to fair terms of social cooperation with the recognition that only the oppressive power of the state, not the free use of reason, can unify society around some single comprehensive religious or ethical doctrine, including individualist views of life. He also held, as we have seen, that working out fair terms of cooperation consists in finding rules of association that people can by their own lights see reason to accept: "reasonable persons ... desire for its own sake a

---

28. Cf. in this regard David Estlund's account of an "undogmatic substantive political liberalism" in *Democratic Authority: A Philosophical Framework* (Princeton, NJ: Princeton University Press, 2008), 57.

social world in which they, as free and equal, can cooperate with others on terms all can accept."[29] This means that being reasonable (in his sense) is tantamount to adhering to his "liberal principle of legitimacy." Yet again, why should fairness, as he understood it, have so fundamental an importance in political life as to determine that the liberal conception of political legitimacy, among so many others, is the correct one? We cannot answer this question unless we go more deeply into the moral underpinnings of that legitimacy principle itself. Only then will it become clear in effect why political liberalism regards it as imperative to go beyond its classical forebears.

In earlier writings, I have argued that this moral basis lies in a certain idea of *respect for persons*.[30] It is crucial, however, to perceive what idea of respect is involved, since there are many different concepts in circulation, some of them entailing comprehensive ethical doctrines of the sort that political liberalism must want to avoid. So I will lay out the argument again, though this time in more detail than before. (The following account should be understood as superseding earlier versions.) For my aim is to make as perspicuous as possible the moral content of the conception of legitimacy on which political liberalism rests.

Let us begin, as before, with Rawls's statement of the liberal principle of legitimacy. What is the basis of the conviction that the fundamental terms of political society should be ones that those whom they are to bind, understanding themselves, as he said, as free and equal—by which he meant, as each endowed with the two moral powers (of developing a sense of justice and a conception of the good) and as each members of the community in their own right, not antecedently subject to the

29. Rawls, *Political Liberalism*, 50.
30. See in particular *Autonomy of Morality*, chapter 6.

authority of another—can see reason to endorse? Do we, for instance, accept this principle (supposing we do) because we think that in general valid moral rules are those rules of conduct that people could not reasonably reject?[31] There are a number of difficulties with this response. One is that the conception of morality to which it appeals looks circular. Do not the reasons to accept the basic rules of morality turn ultimately on the fact that, since they prohibit or enjoin significant ways of harming or benefiting others, it is wrong not to observe them? In other words, is it not the moral rightness of these rules that thus explains why they cannot be reasonably rejected, and not the reverse? Or if that is not so, then does not such an account of morality show an intimate affiliation with those individualist ideals of self-determination to which, for political liberalism, the ground rules of political society need to be neutral? Should we really abstain from judging others by moral rules that they from their perspective would find unacceptable? In any case, whatever the strength of these objections, views about the basis of moral rules in general are not, I believe, the pertinent source of our conviction that political principles must be able to meet with the reasonable agreement of the citizens they are to govern.

---

31. Such a theory of morality is presented in T. M. Scanlon, *What We Owe to Each Other* (Cambridge, MA: Harvard University Press, 1998). He does respond to the circularity objection (4–5, 10–11, 168–70, 391), but unconvincingly, I believe. The distinction he rightly draws between the wrong-making properties of an act (its being an intentional killing, say) and the act being wrong (its being an act of murder) does not suffice to show, it seems to me, that its being wrong consists in being the sort of act one would reasonably reject. On the contrary, only insofar as its being an intentional killing is (part of) what makes it a wrongful act of murder would one reasonably reject any rule that permitted it. For some intentional killings (as in wartime) may be permissible.

That conviction reflects instead the distinctive feature of political principles that sets them apart from the other moral rules to which we hold people accountable, namely that they are *coercive*. Moral rules may be divided into two groups. With some we believe people can be rightly forced to comply if necessary, whereas others we do not regard as valid objects of legal enforcement, whatever disapproval or even outrage we may feel and express when they are violated. The first group alone has the status of political principles. For an association is political insofar as it possesses (or asserts it possesses) the means to secure compliance with its rules by what it claims to be the legitimate use of coercion.[32] Compliance may, of course, be voluntary, and to this extent the rules do not need to be enforced. But as political rules, they remain enforceable, unlike other sorts of moral rules.

By "coercion" I mean, here as elsewhere, precisely the use or threat of force. Social life in general certainly contains other ways as well of shaping behavior, various means of pressure—not least practices of moral praise and blame—that impel people to conform to favored patterns of thought and action. This is not in itself a bad thing (how else, for instance, would people learn the basics of morality?), though it can sometimes, as John Stuart Mill argued in *On Liberty*, stifle valuable forms of individuality. But in either case, social pressure and the use or threat of force are quite different in the sort of power they exert.[33] Social pressure can always, if at some cost, be ignored or combated. Not so with the mechanisms of enforcement at the

---

32. In this I follow Max Weber, *Wirtschaft und Gesellschaft* (Tübingen: Mohr, 1972), I.1.§17. See above, chapter 1, §§3–4.

33. Gerald Gaus seems to me to miss their difference in his critique of my views in "Respect for Persons and Public Justification," in *Respect for Persons*, ed. Richard Dean and Oliver Sensen (New York: Oxford University Press, 2018), 1–23.

disposal of the modern state, which claims, not incidentally, a monopoly on the legitimate use of force. When embodied in custom and prevailing opinion, moral rules enjoy considerable influence over people's lives. But their impact is importantly less constraining than the kind of control those moral rules exercise that have come to figure among the coercive principles of political association. Coercion leaves people with no real alternative to doing what they are being forced to do. This is why the question of permissible coercion plays a crucial role in the liberal idea of legitimacy.[34]

Observe that coercion or the use or threat of force cannot be deemed inherently wrong, for then political association would be impossible. From a political standpoint, the question— indeed the fundamental question—concerns the conditions under which recourse to coercion is justified or legitimate. That is why Rawls's formulation of the liberal principle of legitimacy refers to "the exercise of political power" as what it is intended to govern. And it is why political liberalism, in undertaking a refoundation of the liberal tradition, needs to focus on the concept of legitimacy. Different political systems, to be sure, invoke different sorts of justification—different legitimation stories—for their right to impose, by force if necessary, the rules defining their terms of association. The characteristic

34. A complex case is when the state engages in some symbolic act (speeches, for instance) intended to favor a particular religion or conception of the human good. The social pressure such state favoritism exerts is objectionable from a liberal point of view because this pressure, though not coercive in itself (one may simply ignore the speeches), comes from a state with coercive powers. A private organization engaging in such actions would, after all, be unproblematic. This is why I think Colin Bird is wrong to argue (against me and others) that the liberal idea of political principles having to meet with the reasonable agreement of those subject to them does not have essentially to do with the legitimacy of coercion. See Bird, "Coercion and Public Justification," *Politics, Philosophy, and Economics* 13, no. 3 (2014): 189–214.

claim of a liberal order has always been that its legitimacy in imposing coercive rules of political association stems from its citizens being able to see reason to accept these rules. What, then, to return to our question, are the moral assumptions that underlie this liberal principle, particularly as conceived by political liberalism?

These assumptions have to do, I believe, with an essential feature of what it is to be *a person*. As persons we are, whatever our view of the good, beings essentially capable not only (as are the higher animals too) of thinking and acting for what we take to be reasons, but also of reflecting on such reasons in the sense of examining whether they really do constitute good reasons. Reflection of this sort, let it be noted, is an activity in which we can engage from a variety of standpoints and not solely from a position of critical detachment in which we stand back from inherited forms of life in order to work out for ourselves how we should think and act. People of faith, people imbued with a sense of tradition, can still reflect on the real worth of the reasons their commitments appear to give them—they often cannot help but do so—even if their deliberations take place within the bounds of their guiding assumptions. Nothing in this concept of a person harbors an allegiance to individualist ideals. That does not mean I presume that all reasonable people (in my sense of the term) will necessarily see reason to endorse the concept. As I already remarked several times in the previous chapter, it is not the ambition of political liberalism to build on foundations that no reasonable person will dispute.[35]

---

35. For more on this concept of the person, see "Person und Anerkennung," chapter 3 in my book *Das Selbst in seinem Verhältnis zu sich und zu anderen.*

We are now in a position to grasp the relevant notion of *respect* that, given the problem of legitimate coercion for persons so understood, grounds what I regard as the liberal idea of political legitimacy. Imagine a situation in which we (the state) bring about in others by the threat of force their conformity to a rule of conduct we do not suppose that they too could see reason from their point of view to impose on the community. We would, it is true, be relying on their ability to think and act for what they take to be reasons, for they cannot be moved by threats except by seeing reason to fear what we shall do to them if they fail to comply. But our aim would be only to take advantage of that ability, compelling them thereby to act in a way that advances the ulterior goals we seek to achieve: the establishment of social order, the realization of some public good, even the satisfaction of some interest of theirs they cannot properly pursue themselves. We would not, in imposing that rule on their conduct, be valuing their ability to think and act for reasons as something good in itself. For that would involve subjecting them only to rules by which they could be moved to abide, not by reasons to fear the consequences of noncompliance, but by the reasons for imposing the rules in the first place. And that would mean appealing to their distinctive capacity as persons, namely their ability to reflectively evaluate apparent or purported reasons. If we thus sought to engage their capacity for reflection in getting them to adhere to some rule of conduct, we would be showing this capacity of theirs precisely the same intrinsic regard we have for our own when we propose that rule in virtue of concluding that there are good reasons to enact it. As one might say in echo of Kant, though without the metaphysical obscurities of Kant's ethics and also (unlike him) with an eye only to coercive actions, we would then be treating these persons, in their capacity as rational and reflective beings, no longer solely as means but also as ends. We would, in short, be treating them with respect.[36]

To respect others as persons in their own right when coercion is involved is therefore to require that political principles, or at least the fundamental ones, be justifiable to them from their perspective just as they presumably are to us from ours.[37] (In the next section, I explain the qualification as well as show why this initial formulation needs to be somewhat modified.) We need not suppose the same to hold for those moral principles by which we evaluate others, even strongly disapprove of

36. Because the point is that being subject to coercive rules should be compatible with being shown respect in one's distinctive capacity as a person, it will not suffice that we simply try our best to explain to others that they have from their perspective reason to accept some such rule. That is the view of respect defended by Christopher Eberle in *Religious Conviction in Liberal Politics* (Cambridge: Cambridge University Press, 2002), criticizing my conception (120–28) as well as that of others, and it allows him to say that if we fail in that effort but believe we have from our own perspective good reason to endorse the rule, we are entitled to impose it anyway. This seems to me a recipe for a very illiberal politics. The liberal idea of legitimacy, I believe, is that coercion itself should square with respect. That means that the principles of political association must be in fact justifiable to those whom they are to bind.

37. David Enoch is right, in his critique of political liberalism ("Against Public Reason," *Oxford Studies in Political Philosophy* 1 [Oxford: Oxford University Press, 2015], 111–42), that such a requirement involves treating people in this regard as equals. But the idea of equality involved is not, as he supposes, one that forbids giving more weight to our reasons to impose the principles than to what may be their reasons to reject them. Against such a view he objects that it is the reasons themselves for imposing certain principles, and not whose reasons they are, that should matter. However, the idea of equality involved, at least in political liberalism as I conceive it, has to do with the conditions under which persons may rightly be subject to coercive principles, conditions that state (with qualifications I shall later add) that *each* person must be able to see reasons why these principles should be imposed.

how they may act, yet do so without appealing to the state's means of coercion. Those principles, we may believe, are morally binding on them, whether or not they can see reason to accept them. Why should a commitment to liberalism inhibit our powers of moral judgment? But the use or threat of force is different, since it consists in compelling people to do what they otherwise would not do, and it would, if unconstrained by the norm of respect, involve treating them, in their capacity as rational and reflective beings, merely in an instrumental way. To be legitimate, so this principle of respect asserts, the use or threat of force must accord with the reason of the citizens themselves who are potentially subject to it.

Respect for persons in this sense forms, then, the ultimate moral basis of the liberal conception of political legitimacy. It is the source of the principle, as I myself will now provisionally formulate it, that the fundamental terms of political association are legitimate only if those whom they are to bind can see from their perspective reason (again, not necessarily the same reason) to accept them. To this whole account, centered as it is on reasonable disagreement and agreement, one might perhaps object that a liberal regime should treat people with respect even when they fail to be reasonable. That is true. Yet it too has its place in this account. Though the central problem for the liberal tradition has been the definition of political legitimacy given the tendency of reasonable people to disagree about the nature of the human good, the conception of respect in which the solution lies covers equally those whose ethical and religious views may not by their own lights be well reasoned out. For the basic terms of political association need to be ones they too could see reason to accept, were they to be reasoning appropriately from their point of view. When, indeed, individuals fail to grasp what political principles their views in fact give them reason to endorse, how else are they to be treated with respect except by holding them to be subject, even then, to those principles alone which they could, if thinking more clearly from their point of departure, see reason to accept?[38] That is precisely what this conception of respect implies. For as I have stressed all along, the question is not what political principles people do, but rather what principles they can from their perspective see reason to endorse.

The concept of respect for persons I have outlined is not, to be sure, the only sense the notion of respect can have. Nor is it all that we might understand by respect in a comprehensive moral theory. But it is the principle that lies at the foundations of a liberal conception of political society.[39] It is, in particular, the principle on which political liberalism relies in arguing that the individualist assumptions of its predecessors should be

38. Steven Wall ("Perfectionism, Reasonableness, and Respect," *Political Theory* 42, no. 4 [August 2014]: 468–89) tries to use this sort of situation as a wedge to argue that respect also requires holding people to be subject to political principles that errors of "soundness" in their comprehensive beliefs themselves keep them from acknowledging (473–76). But this (intentionally perfectionist) conclusion does not follow, nor is it clear from Wall's account who exactly gets to determine what count as "sound" conceptions of the good.

39. Rawls himself showed a great reluctance to admit that a principle of respect lies at the basis of liberal thought, largely because of the many different meanings the idea of "respect" can have. At the end of *A Theory of Justice* (Cambridge, MA: Harvard University Press, 1971), for instance, he declared that he had not sought to derive his principles of justice from the notion of respect for persons because that very notion calls for interpretation, which only a conception of justice can provide (585–86). The hermeneutic point is well taken. But it does not rule out the possibility that respect, in a sense to be grasped only in the light of his theory as a whole, is a value on which that theory substantively depends. We may have to rely on our thinking about justice or about political legitimacy in order to determine the appropriate sense of "respect" they embody. Yet the principle of respect for persons, thus delimited, may still form the moral foundation of the doctrines themselves.

abandoned. For not only does this idea of respect, as I explained, carry no allegiance to individualist views of life; it also requires, given the persistence of reasonable disagreement about such views, that they play no role in shaping the basic rules of political society.

Since then political liberalism builds upon this moral foundation, we would be wrong to think it accords respect for persons (so understood) the political significance it does because citizens can all see reason for doing so. That supposition is not in fact likely to be true. Reasonable people in my sense of the term—exercising their general capacities of reason in good faith and to the best of their abilities—need not, depending on their beliefs and interests, be able to recognize any reason to think that coercive principles should be rationally acceptable to those whom they bind. They may on the contrary find themselves justified in rejecting that notion if they believe, for instance, that the most important feature of political society is that it be pleasing to God. Of course, if "reasonable" is understood in Rawls's moral sense of being committed to seeking fair principles of cooperation, then such people will be, as I have explained, well on their way to seeing good reason to believe that political principles must respect those whom they are to bind. But that is a different matter. And as I remarked near the end of the preceding section, it is best not to use the term "reasonable" as Rawls does, since then an important moral assumption is not being made explicit.

No, respect for persons has the position in political liberalism it does, not because it constitutes common ground and forms an object of reasonable agreement, but because it is what directs us in the first place to look for common ground, to seek the principles of our political life in the area of reasonable agreement. Thus, political liberalism does not aim at correcting the individualism of its classical antecedents simply because individualist views of human flourishing have shown themselves to be eminently controversial. Their disputability is seen as calling for such a revision only in virtue of an underlying commitment to the principle of respect.

4. Implications and Prospects

The liberal conception of political legitimacy, given what seems to me the best understanding of liberalism's deepest motivations, rests therefore on the concept of respect I have described. This fact has a number of important implications.

A first implication is that in a liberal regime the norm of respect and the principle of legitimacy it grounds do not have the same sort of standing as the basic political or constitutional principles worked out on their basis. Insofar as those principles are able to be the object of reasonable agreement, their political validity can be said to derive from the collective will of the citizens. But the same is not true of the norm of respect and thus of the liberal conception of legitimacy. They must be understood as having a deeper kind of validity. To be sure, the legitimacy principle is political in character since its requirement that the terms of political life be reasonably acceptable to all is itself meant to be enforceable. But unlike the other political principles it serves to justify, it does not draw its bindingness from citizens being able to see a reason to endorse it. It must be regarded as a principle binding on citizens independently of their collective will, enjoying an authority they have not fashioned themselves. For only in recognizing its independent validity are they moved to give their political existence the consensual shape they intend it to have. At the fundamental level, citizens of a liberal democracy cannot therefore, contrary to

Jürgen Habermas, regard themselves as the authors of the laws to which they are subject.[40] I have been arguing that the liberal conception of political legitimacy rests on the idea of respect for persons. But what, one may ask, is the source of the validity of that idea itself? What, in other words, are the deeper values or principles on which it in turn rests? I do not have an answer to this question. But I caution that we should not suppose there must be one. At some point, justification comes to an end, and we must recognize that certain principles ultimately speak for themselves. Respect for persons, as I have defined it, may be a principle of just that sort. It depends on persons having the distinctive features I have mentioned. But it may not depend as well on any deeper moral principle. It may constitute instead an example what I called in chapter 1, §7, an "ultimate though fact-dependent principle." In any case, my aim here is to point out the foundational role that respect plays in political liberalism and the consequences that follow from this role.

Now a second, quite important implication is that the idea of respect must define the very nature of the agreement (to use this term for ease of exposition) that according to the liberal principle of legitimacy determines what political principles may be instituted.[41] To see this, observe first that agreement in this

40. Jürgen Habermas, *Faktizität und Geltung* (Frankfurt: Suhrkamp, 1992), 51–52, 135, 153. As the early French liberal critics of Rousseau recognized, popular sovereignty or the democratic will must be understood as subject to certain basic rights of the individual. See, for instance, Benjamin Constant, *Principes de politique* (1815), Chapitre premier: "La souveraineté [du people] n'existe que d'une manière limitée et relative. Au point où commencent l'indépendance et l'existence individuelle, s'arrête la juridiction de cette souveraineté" (*Œuvres* [Paris: Gallimard, 1957], 1071).

41. The following condition on the agreement in question is therefore far from being ad hoc, contrary to what David Enoch claims is typical of such "idealizations" in various versions of political liberalism. See his essay "Against Public Reason," 117–30.

case is manifestly a normative notion, if only because it means reasonable, not simply actual agreement. Political life, from the liberal standpoint, is to be based on principles that citizens, despite their various moral, religious, and metaphysical beliefs, can from their different perspectives see reason to accept. Though what they can see reason to accept depends on their existing beliefs and interests, these reasons must be, for the system to be legitimate, reasons they really have, not reasons they merely think they have. However, reasonableness in this sense is not the sole standard or constraint governing the agreement in question. Because the idea of respect for persons is what requires the search for common ground, it must figure as a further condition that political principles have to satisfy if they are to count as being the object of a legitimating agreement among citizens. In other words, the terms of political society are to be judged by reference to what citizens would accept, were they not only reasonable but also committed to the norm of respect for persons.

This means that the conception of legitimacy lying at the heart of political liberalism should be formulated more precisely as follows: *The fundamental principles of political society, being coercive in nature, ought to be such that all who are subject to them must be able from their perspective to see reason (not necessarily the same reason) to endorse them on the assumption— perhaps for some of them counterfactual* (I will come back to the import of this clause)—*that they are committed to the idea of respect for persons and thus to basing political association on principles that can meet with the reasonable agreement of citizens.* The constraint that the idea of respect thus places on reasonable agreement as the basis of legitimate political principles is implicit in Rawls's own statement of the liberal principle of legitimacy. For recall that, in his formulation, the exercise of political power is justifiable only if it rests on principles acceptable to all citizens insofar as they are, he stipulated, "rational and reasonable," and what he meant by "reasonable," as we have seen, is being disposed to seek fair terms of cooperation, that is, terms justifiable to all. Yet the moral content of the constraint lies hidden in Rawls's formulations. I believe clarity is served by bringing it out explicitly.

These two implications of the role of respect help us to see, thirdly, how to respond to a frequent objection to political liberalism. Ideas of social justice, it is often objected, are no less subject to reasonable disagreement than ideas of the good, and therefore the search for principles of political association to which all citizens can reasonably agree must come to naught.[42] This objection rests, however, on several misunderstandings, at least if political liberalism is understood as I have proposed. To begin with, there is the fact that political liberalism's primary concern should be seen as lying with the question of legitimacy, and only secondarily with social or distributive justice. But also, it is wrong to suppose that its aim is to develop either a concept of justice or a conception of legitimacy that is uncontroversial. Its conceptions of justice do have a different function than conceptions of the human good: they define the framework of rules and institutions in which people may pursue their various and sometimes conflicting ideas of what is good and gives life meaning. Such a framework, according to political liberalism, is legitimately instituted if it rests upon the idea of respect for persons, and that idea requires, as we have now seen, that the fundamental principles of political society be ones that citizens can see reason to endorse on the assumption that

---

42. See, for instance, Jeremy Waldron, *Law and Disagreement* (Oxford: Oxford University Press, 1999), 105–6, 112, and chapter 7.

they accept this idea of respect. Yet at the same time one should acknowledge, as I noted at the end of the last section, that some citizens may see from their perspective no reason to accept that idea. Political liberalism ought to be under no illusions on this score. It should not expect that all citizens or people generally will be able to see in the light of their deepest interests and convictions reason to endorse its defining principles. It is naïve to suppose that any idea of political legitimacy, given the diversity of views about the good and the right, can be in this sense universally justified. Political liberalism is exceptional, I believe, in its recognition of how fundamental a problem reasonable disagreement about moral matters poses for political life. In this regard, it sees clearly the key difference between political and moral philosophy. But the solution it proposes cannot claim to transcend such disagreement altogether.

This view resembles what Jonathan Quong has advanced as an "internal" conception of political liberalism. Yet I am unhappy with the way he describes this conception, as when he asserts,

> The aim is not to justify liberalism to a radically diverse constituency, one that may include people who reject liberalism's most fundamental values. Rather, the aim is to understand how liberal rights and institutions can be publicly justified to the constituency of an ideal democratic society.[43]

Though political liberalism must certainly explain how citizens who hold liberal values can do so compatibly with disagreeing about so much else, it is crucial to remember that liberalism in general and political liberalism in particular have taken shape

43. Jonathan Quong, *Liberalism without Perfection* (Oxford: Oxford University Press, 2011), 6.

as a response to a problem of "radical diversity" or of what I have been calling, more precisely, reasonable disagreement about the good and the right.[44] Quong tends to proceed as though the liberal tradition already exists, the question being whether its guiding ideals and assumptions can be shown to be internally coherent. But the deeper question is why it exists at all, what problem it has arisen in order to solve. Without an answer to that question, we cannot understand its underlying motivations, which are what I have been trying to bring out.[45] Still, it is true—on this Quong is right—the solution it offers is not one that can necessarily be justified to all reasonable people, understood as people exercising their rational faculties about moral questions sincerely and to the best of their abilities. In this, it is unexceptional since every political conception excludes, a point to which I return shortly.

Now it is true that reasonable people who stand opposed to the very notion of a liberal society will still be obliged, by force if necessary, to comply with its rules even though they may see no reason to endorse their basis or some of the rules themselves.

44. Quong goes so far as to assert that on the internal conception "pluralism [he means reasonable disagreement, CL] is not a fact about the world which liberal theory must accommodate. Rather, pluralism is to be understood to be a consequence of liberalism itself" (ibid., 139; also 142). Though it is true, as I mentioned earlier, that liberal ideas of toleration have helped to expand the breadth of reasonable disagreement, they originally emerged as a response to reasonable disagreement about the nature of the human good.

45. This is why I think it a mistake for Martha Nussbaum ("Perfectionist Liberalism," 20) to want to discard from political liberalism its reliance on the idea of reasonableness in the epistemic sense. One thereby loses a sense of the problem to which political liberalism is a response. One also cannot make sense of the fact, noted toward the end of the preceding section, that the liberal conception of legitimacy refers to reasons that citizens could see from their perspective, whether they do so or not, to endorse various political principles.

But this, as my more precise formulation of the liberal legitimacy principle suggests, is not so much to fail to respect them
as it is to compel them to act in accord with the rules of a political community that they have a role in shaping as well, inasmuch as these rules must be ones that they could see reason to
endorse if, the rest of their beliefs remaining unchanged, they
accepted the idea of respect. They are thereby given a qualified
kind of respect.

There is more to say on this last score. But I want first to
point out another source of continual disagreement about
what is just. It is the fact that the liberal principle of legitimacy
does not determine one single conception of distributive justice. As noted earlier (§3), it serves as a constraint, delimiting
a range of eligible understandings, what Rawls himself called
"the family of liberal conceptions."[46] So it is to be expected
that a liberal society will be home to an ongoing debate, within
such bounds, about the specific character of social justice.[47]
On some basic rights and freedoms the different conceptions
will agree, and insofar as these matters appear to be required by
the very idea of respect, they should be the object of constitutional guarantees. Yet political decisions must be made that go
beyond these points of agreement, and here the different liberal conceptions are bound to come into conflict. That is why I
have been saying that the idea of respect directly governs only
the *fundamental* principles of political society.

But it is also why one of those principles must determine
how such further matters—whether they concern questions

46. Rawls, *Political Liberalism*, xlviii, 6, 223.

47. As I also indicated earlier, it is to be expected as well that different liberal
societies, as they come to make respect for persons their guiding commitment, will
develop as a result of their specific historical experience somewhat different inter-
pretations of what it entails for the constitution of a just society.

of policy or the concrete interpretation of constitutional guarantees—are to be settled. The idea of respect, requiring that political principles be reasonably acceptable to all, entails that normally questions of the first, policy sort should be settled on the basis of democratic procedures (e.g., elections, universal suffrage, majority voting) since all citizens then have an equal say, none being invidiously supposed to be wiser or more virtuous than others. In this way, citizens who disagree with the laws thus enacted, but with which they must still comply, are shown respect indirectly insofar as these procedures themselves are ones that they, if committed to the idea of respect, can see reason to accept. To this extent, then, political liberalism entails the institution of democratic self-rule.[48] Questions of the second sort, precisely because they can involve the protection of individuals in fundamental regards from the will of the majority, are different, however. Here a concern for respect may well be taken to recommend such nondemocratic procedures as judicial review and constitutional courts.

I now return to the fact that a commitment to respect for persons may not form part of every citizen's thinking or be a commitment every citizen, given his or her present perspective, can see reason to adopt. The belief that the coercive principles of political association should be justifiable to those whom they are to bind is perhaps so widespread in modern liberal societies as often—in many circles—to go without saying. But it was not so in the past. And today too it is rejected, perhaps most notoriously, by those (of whom there are many not only in parts of the world other than the West) who believe that in the political realm conformity to God's will overrides

---

48. Here I am indebted to the David Estlund's account of the "default" status of democratic self-rule. See his *Democratic Authority*, 36–38, 221–22.

respect for human reason.[49] It is also rejected by those who, wedded to certain ethical ideals, believe a state that fails to devote itself to fostering virtue and excellence, as they conceive them, is unworthy of allegiance. In virtue of the natural tendency to reasonable disagreement about moral matters, we should not be surprised that so many refuse in good faith to accept the liberal vision of political life and regard its form of political rule as illegitimate.

Thus, we need to recognize candidly—here a fourth crucial implication of the foundational role of respect for persons— that the inclusiveness to which liberal societies must aspire also excludes. It denies that the basic terms of political life need to be justifiable to citizens who, rejecting the relevant idea of respect, do not see the same value in the project of seeking common ground amidst reasonable disagreement about the human good and the meaning of life. That modern liberalism cannot escape involving exclusion is a fact that liberal thinkers and citizens alike have sometimes been reluctant to acknowledge. From its beginnings in the early modern struggle for religious toleration to the present day, the liberal tradition has sought to build despite people's differences a truly inclusive community. It has at times forgotten that every principle of political inclusion, however broad-minded it may be, constitutes a principle of exclusion as well. For every such principle embodies values that some individuals will reject and consequently defines a community from whose spirit they are shut out or in which they must feel like strangers. This is the important truth that the brilliant though authoritarian German theorist Carl

49. This perspective is to be distinguished from the religious view, very influential in the historical development of liberal thought, that God's will is that political society take shape in accord with human reason.

Schmitt discerned, among so much else he got wrong, when he declared that political society depends essentially on a distinction between friend and enemy.[50] No political conception, not even political liberalism for all its desire for accommodation, can prove agreeable to every view of the human good or of what gives life meaning. Liberal societies are bound to contain some whose beliefs make them unable to see themselves—as I have argued liberal citizens must—as part of a "people" united by their historical experience, mutual trust, and respect for persons in endorsing the basics of individual freedom, equality, and democratic self-government.

The liberal aim cannot therefore be, as I observed already in the previous chapter (§4), to bring about a general reconciliation of individual liberty and political authority. That is impossible.[51] Though political regimes must seek legitimacy

---

50. Carl Schmitt, *Der Begriff des Politischen* (Munich: Duncker & Humblot, 1932).

51. Rousseau held that devising a form of association that reconciles political authority with the liberty of each citizen is the "fundamental problem" of politics (*Du contrat social*, I.6, in *Oeuvres complètes* [Paris: Gallimard, 1964], 3:360). This problem is insoluble, contrary to what many liberal thinkers—such as recently Gerald Gaus (*The Order of Public Reason* [Cambridge: Cambridge University Press, 2011], 1–2, 446)—have believed. Gaus's "public reason liberalism" holds that people reasoning solely on the basis of their various moral perspectives can all come to agree, not indeed on any one code of authoritative social rules, but rather on an "eligible set" of such codes, and that the course of history, the weight of the status quo, and the exercise of power will then steer them toward convergence upon a single member of this set (402–3, 416–18, 425–26, 455). However, this supposed reconciliation of liberty and authority is implausible. Some people's moral perspectives will give them reason to believe that the course of history should be reversed, the status quo resisted, or the exercise of power contested (see above chapter 2, §8). The liberal project, I believe, must instead be to reconcile political authority with the liberty of those committed to certain fundamental moral principles, in particular the principle of respect for persons. This will entail, as I have emphasized, that some people will therefore find themselves excluded and unable to assent freely

in order to carry out their basic function of containing deep-seated conflicts and ensuring the conditions of social coopera-tion, they cannot hope that their legitimation story will escape being reasonably disputed and rejected by some who find them-selves under their rule. Their goal must be to institute a polit-ical order that practices the right kind of exclusion—which means, from the liberal standpoint, one that rests on the prin-ciple of respect for persons, holding itself therefore account-able only to those who are committed to regulating the politi-cal use of coercion by that very principle. In the past as also today, liberal democracies have indeed been wrong to exclude in different ways various groups of people from equal mem-bership in the political community. But there is a fundamental kind of exclusion it is not regrettable but rather necessary that they practice.[52]

At the same time, it is important to realize that those who must feel excluded in a liberal order should not, according to political liberalism, feel excluded altogether. It is not the en-tirety of their beliefs and interests that is refused recognition or allowed no weight in defining the shape of political society, but only that part of their outlook that entails a rejection of the liberal idea of respect for persons. Honoring the spirit of that idea, seeking as far as possible to keep the use of coercion

---

to the rules in force. Not even liberalism, for all its concern for individual liberty, can constitute a solution to Rousseau's problem.

52. Here I disagree with Charles Taylor, who appears to believe that every sort of exclusion to which liberal democracies, in their need to have a "political identity," are prone is to be regretted. Precisely because principles of inclusion must also ex-clude, democratic exclusion is not necessarily, as he supposes, a "dilemma." See "Democratic Exclusion (and Its Remedies?)," chapter 7 in his *Dilemmas and Con-nections* (Cambridge, MA: Harvard University Press, 2011).

within the bounds of what those who are subject to it can see reason to accept, requires therefore (as in my final statement of the liberal conception of legitimacy) ensuring that the basic principles of political life be justifiable to such people as well, on the assumption—counterfactual in their case—that they too held this sort of respect to be a fundamental commitment, but given everything else in their present perspective that they could, compatibly with that, continue to affirm. Though political liberalism, like every political conception, inevitably excludes, it also includes the excluded in a qualified way, and not merely as outsiders to be abided (as other conceptions may do), but as citizens with a role to play in shaping the terms of association. In this regard, which is not the least of its appeals, it is, I think, unique among forms of political exclusion.

I cannot, however, end this chapter on so positive a note. There remains a worry, connected with the point with which I began, about whether political liberalism is able to meet the challenges of the contemporary world. Liberalism in general, I observed, is by its nature and in its self-understanding a latecomer in the history of political conceptions. In explaining that point, I signaled an important assumption in the liberal project of detaching the rules of political society from substantive religious and ethical premises and recasting them as a body of abstract principles, including first and foremost respect for persons and then the principles of freedom, equality, and democratic self-government that stem from it. For that project to succeed, I argued, the citizens of a liberal society—those, that is, whose beliefs do not make them feel excluded—must still regard themselves as forming one people, bound together by a common life that is rooted now primarily in habit, language, and historical experience, if they are to be willing to accept the vulnerabilities that come with adhering to the terms of political association. Not by accident, liberalism developed in tandem with the modern nation-state.

The question, however, is whether this underlying assumption is still realistic and whether the liberal tradition, including political liberalism, has the resources to deal with the salient problems of our time. In a world dominated by a rampant globalized capitalism and hurtling, not unconnectedly, toward environmental disaster, the idea of distinct peoples and sovereign nation-states appears to be increasingly a thing of the past. States find themselves more and more the prisoner of worldwide financial markets and multinational corporations. The new digital technology of the media and the Internet, an integral part of the dynamics of international capital, acts to homogenize cultural differences and to erase historical memory with the immediacy of information (as well as rumor) and entertainment on command. Among those most hurt by the economic consequences of these developments—so particularly among members of the working class—there have arisen xenophobic and authoritarian reactions that have done much to weaken liberal democracies throughout the Western world, but nothing to contain the forces responsible for their distress. Meanwhile, the air thickens, the ice-packs melt, the seas rise, and existing nation-states, such as they are, seem an irrelevance, if not indeed an obstacle, to any way of averting the impending catastrophe.

Some have thought that the solution to these global problems lies in globalizing the liberal perspective, in working out theories of global justice. I am not convinced. Political principles of an abstract liberal character, whatever may be the scale of their deployment, are viable only if the people to be bound by them already share feelings of mutual trust and regard them selves as sharing in a common life. It is not clear that humanity can ever form a people in this sense. Governments have not intervened (if at all) to protect persecuted or terrorized groups elsewhere simply by respect for "human rights," independently of finding it in their own interest to insert themselves into the affairs of another state. I suspect that similarly conceptions of global justice, whatever their moral merits, have a chance of being implemented only if states, liberal states, find themselves impelled to put them into practice. Yet how likely is that in the present age? Some of the most distinctive problems of our world are not among the problems for which liberalism was devised, and they threaten its very viability. Its prospects, I am sad to say, are accordingly uncertain.

Many liberal thinkers have supposed that liberalism and capitalism go hand in hand; others have imagined that liberal principles can limit the excesses of a capitalist economy. But I consider capitalism's insatiable pursuit of economic growth—that is, of profit—to constitute in the long run a mortal danger for the workability of liberal principles, if not indeed for the future of mankind itself.

Conclusion

THIS HAS NOT been an optimistic book. The final paragraphs of the preceding chapter, with their dark picture of the difficulties facing liberal democracy, are by themselves proof of that. But I have also argued more generally that political philosophy should understand its domain to be one in which things are never likely to be as we think they ideally should, in which success is always relative, never complete, and reasons for encouragement are accompanied by signs of trouble. There are two connected themes that have shaped the realistic approach to political philosophy I have defended, an approach that intersects with lines of thinking that today often go indeed under the name of "political realism."

One theme has been *the disharmony of reason and its political consequences*. When dealing with questions having to do with the human good or social justice, reasonable people— that is, people reasoning in good faith and to the best of their abilities—tend naturally to arrive at different and even opposing views. This has not been the understanding in much of the philosophical tradition. Its conviction has been that reason serves to overcome disagreement. When we find ourselves at odds about some ethical matter, reasoning it out together will supposedly lead us to converge on a common view, if only to agree that we lack the means to decide the issue. Experience, however, suggests the contrary. Careful reflection about such questions, once it moves beyond platitudes and gets into details, is more likely to augment our differences than to diminish them. Agreement, when it occurs, is all too often a sign of inattention or inhibition. Why this should be so is not hard to explain. Reasoning always takes place against a background of existing beliefs, standards, and interests, and though we can come to see reasons to modify certain elements among our starting points, these reasons depend on other background elements that remain constant, at least at the time. Because different life histories are bound to give people different assumptions about how to approach ethical questions, they are therefore likely to arrive at different conclusions, particularly when—as is the case with such questions—key concepts can be variously interpreted and crucial considerations variously weighted. Reasonable disagreement is to be expected.

It may be individuals who disagree. It may also be groups, shaped by different moral or religious traditions and engaged in different practices and ways of life. In both cases, reasonable disagreement constitutes a formidable political problem, since it forms one of the principal sources of conflict that imperil the possibility of social order and cooperation. Now any system of political rule must undertake above all to devise and impose authoritative rules for handling the most important conflicts in its society, including therefore those that arise from reasonable disagreement about the good and the right. This fact shows that the primary concern of any political order—and thus the fundamental concept with which political philosophy must deal—cannot be social justice. How the benefits and burdens of social cooperation should be distributed is precisely one of the enduring objects of controversy and thus a major source of social conflict. Before that question can be addressed, the very possibility of social cooperation must be secured. The primary concern must therefore lie, as I have argued, with the question of legitimacy instead. For the rules or laws a state imposes will carry authority (as opposed to being simply commands one is forced to obey) and social cooperation will be thereby assured, only if people in the society by and large regard them as to some degree legitimately, that is, justifiably imposed. Any state must accordingly seek to legitimate its exercise of power in the eyes of those it governs if it is to carry out successfully its basic task of bringing social conflict under control.

Certainly, ideals of social justice inspire. States typically claim to pursue them, and political philosophy has found it inspiring to develop systematic theories of distributive justice. But justice in political life must always be subordinate to legitimacy. However great may be the intrinsic merits of some idea of justice, a state must still provide some justification of its right to impose it on those who may disagree with it, just as we too must do if we are thinking politically, however much we may believe it is the correct view of justice. Even if one holds that its intrinsic merits justify its imposition, this goes beyond simply reiterating those merits and amounts to a conception of why it may, with all the coercive means at the state's disposal, be legitimately imposed.

There have been, historically, many different conceptions of political legitimacy, each of them specifying (these are the three components of the idea of legitimacy I distinguished in chapter 1, §5) the right with which some political order wields coercive power, the areas of social life in which it may exercise it, and the people over whom it rightly has jurisdiction. Liberalism rests on one such conception. Its core, I argued, involves an idea of respect for persons and can be formulated in the following terms: The fundamental principles of political society, being coercive in nature, ought to be such that all who are subject to them must be able from their point of view to see reason to endorse them, assuming a commitment—which some may in fact not have—to basing political association on principles that can meet with the reasonable agreement of all.

At this point, however, a second realistic theme of this book comes into play: *the permanence of conflict.* Conceptions of political legitimacy depend, not only on various factual beliefs, but also—something that contemporary "political realists" with their wholesale rejection of "a morality prior to politics" often overlook—on certain moral principles, in particular principles having to do with the justifiable exercise of coercive power. These principles especially are bound to be such that some people, carefully reflecting to the best of their abilities, will see reason from their perspective to question or reject them. In other words, reasonable disagreement not only sets one of the main problems to which political rule aims to be the solution. It also extends to the solution devised. For this difficulty there can be no complete remedy. Every conception of political legitimacy, however inclusive it aims to be, also excludes. Liberalism is no exception. For some people's view of the world will move them to believe that the most important thing about any system of political rule is not whether it respects the reason of those it governs, but instead whether it conforms to God's will or fosters excellence of character (as they of course understand it). Such people are and must feel excluded by the basic terms of a liberal society. There can be no general reconciliation between individual liberty and political authority. The appeal of liberalism must ultimately lie in the worth of the principles by which it both practices inclusion and also excludes.

Unlike much of contemporary political philosophy, this book has not then developed some vision of social justice or explored the virtues of democratic inclusiveness. I have indeed defended a certain view of liberal democracy. However, I have presented political liberalism as at bottom an account of political legitimacy. And I have been keen to bring out how controversial its assumptions may be and also how problematic its future prospects. The thought has sometimes crossed my mind that the somber tone of this book may reflect the period in which it was written. We live at a time when liberal democracies are beset by populist demagogues, proclaiming that they alone represent the one will of the "real citizens" and scapegoating elites and ethnic minorities as enemies of the people.[1] It is a time when nearly every day gives further evidence of the disintegration of the American political system. As I indicated earlier (chapter 2, §7) in mentioning the essential role played by genocide and slavery, I have no patience with the myth of American exceptionalism. Ultimately everything ends or dies— not just individuals, but republics too.

Yet this book is not simply an expression of my present mood. I have tried to stand back from political philosophy as usually practiced and examine what its fundamental tasks ought to be. This has meant looking at the abiding features of political existence itself—what I have called the circumstances of politics. They consist in the ubiquity of conflicting interests and ideals that, fueled not just by passion or ignorance but by the exercise of reason too, must limit if not extinguish the possibilities of social cooperation unless authoritative rules or laws are established. It follows that the basic concern of both political

1. See the fine analysis in Jan-Werner Müller, *What Is Populism?* (Philadelphia: University of Pennsylvania Press, 2016).

life and political philosophy must lie with the question of legitimacy, that is, with the question of who is entitled to institute these rules, what scope they may have, and over whom they should have sway. There is, to be sure, a place in political philosophy for theories of the good society. But it is a circumscribed place. Political philosophy differs from moral philosophy in having to deal with the social problems that arise from the fact that people—reasonable people—are bound to disagree about what constitutes the good society. To this extent, it is a more reflective enterprise.

INDEX

America, 118, 128, 176
Aquinas, Thomas, 66
Aristotle, 1, 6, 29–31, 33, 35–36, 39, 40,
    41, 48, 57
authority, 4–5, 15, 20–21, 23, 28, 33, 34,
    38, 40, 57, 67, 95, 98–99, 102, 105,
    108–10, 127; definition of, 8, 41–42,
    43–44, 82, 84–85, 90–91, 173–74;
    and liberty, 50, 167–68, 175. See
    also legitimacy: as distinct from
    authority

Bayle, Pierre, 9, 125
Berlin, Isaiah, 140
Besson, Samantha, 137n15
Bird, Colin, 151n
Böckenförde, Ernst-Wolfgang, 127
Bodin, Jean, 9, 125

capitalism, 118, 128, 132, 170, 171
Christensen, David, 136n13
Christianity, 6–7, 31–32, 124. See also
    religion
coercion, 12, 20, 22, 32, 44, 46, 49, 75,
    119, 145, 150–51, 153–54, 168, 175
Cohen, G. A., 22–23, 50–66
consent, 87, 95, 112–19, 146
Constant, Benjamin, 131, 159n40
constructivism, 59–60
contextualism. See justification
cooperation, social, 4–5, 33, 44, 68,
    79–83, 85, 88–89, 91, 102, 105, 115–17,
    120, 127, 173–74, 176

Dante, 6
democracy, 14, 120, 158–59, 165, 168n
Deneen, Patrick J., 130n8
Descartes, René, 1
disagreement. See reasonable
    disagreement
Dworkin, Ronald, 114n

Eberle, Christopher, 154n36
Enoch, David, 139n17, 154n37, 159n41
Estlund, David, 58n28, 147n, 165n
exclusion. See inclusion and exclusion

Fawcett, Edmund, 14
Finley, M. I., 103n

Galileo, 66
Galston, William, 71n
Gaus, Gerald, 150n33, 167n51
Geuss, Raymond, 13n, 73n5
God, 16, 77, 85, 106, 120, 147, 157, 165,
    120, 147, 175. See also religion
Goldman, Alvin, 137n15

Habermas, Jürgen, 107n, 158–59
Hall, Edward, 93n25, 106n
history: importance of, 16, 26–28, 41,
    57, 89, 99–104, 106–7, 111, 123, 132,
    167n51; and memory, 126, 127, 170
Hobbes, Thomas, 29, 33–34, 38–39,
    41–42, 68, 125; on reasonable dis-
    agreement, 7, 9, 35, 36, 74, 83
Hume, David, 81–82, 113, 118n44

A NOTE ON THE TYPE

This book has been composed in Arno, an Old-style
serif typeface in the classic Venetian tradition,
designed by Robert Slimbach at Adobe.